# THE RESEARCH FUNDING TOOLKIT

# THE
# RESEARCH
# FUNDING
# TOOLKIT

JACQUELINE ALDRIDGE & ANDREW M DERRINGTON

Los Angeles | London | New Delhi
Singapore | Washington DC

Los Angeles | London | New Delhi
Singapore | Washington DC

SAGE Publications Ltd
1 Oliver's Yard
55 City Road
London EC1Y 1SP

SAGE Publications Inc.
2455 Teller Road
Thousand Oaks, California 91320

SAGE Publications India Pvt Ltd
B 1/I 1 Mohan Cooperative Industrial Area
Mathura Road
New Delhi 110 044

SAGE Publications Asia-Pacific Pte Ltd
3 Church Street
#10-04 Samsung Hub
Singapore 049483

**Library of Congress Control Number: 2011941451**

**British Library Cataloguing in Publication data**

A catalogue record for this book is available from
the British Library

Editor: Katie Metzler
Editorial assistant: Anna Horvai
Production editor: Ian Antcliff
Copyeditor: Sarah Bury
Proofreader: Louise Harnby
Marketing manager: Ben Griffin-Sherwood
Cover design: Lisa Harper
Typeset by: C&M Digitals (P) Ltd
Printed and bound by CPI Group Ltd,
Croydon, CRO 4YY

MIX
Paper from
responsible sources
FSC® C013604

ISBN 978-0-85702-967-6
ISBN 978-0-85702-968-3 (pbk)

# Contents

# ABOUT THE AUTHORS

**Jacqueline Aldridge** is Research Manager at Kent Business School and has worked in research administration for eight years. During that time, she has helped researchers at all career stages and from a wide range of disciplines write fundable research proposals for a large variety of funding agencies. Before that, she worked in public relations and marketing in blue chip companies and the media industry.

**Andrew Derrington** is Executive Pro Vice Chancellor of Humanities and Social Sciences at the University of Liverpool and has lectured and researched in Psychology at the Universities of Sussex, Newcastle, Nottingham and Kent. His research studies how the brain processes visual information.

Over several years he wrote two successful columns in the *Financial Times*. The Nature of Things, was about science – from astrophysics to zoology. Psych Yourself Up was a guide to the different kinds of psychotherapy available in the UK.

His first research grant was a Beit Memorial fellowship for Medical Research, which he obtained in 1978. His research was continuously funded by fellowships, project and programme grants for the next 30 years.

He served on research grant committees for several UK research councils and the Wellcome Trust. The approach to grant writing that is developed in this book is based on his analysis of how grants' committees make funding decisions.

# ACKNOWLEDGEMENTS

*The Research Funding Toolkit* is based on a grant-writing workshop format created by Prof. Andrew Derrington. It was further developed within the ongoing Grants Factory seminar series at the University of Kent and in the Faculty of Humanities and Social Sciences at the University of Liverpool.

Consequently, much of the advice and guidance in this book has been refined and tested by all the workshop leaders, participants, administrators and managers involved. We would like to thank them all for their support and enthusiasm. It is not possible to list everyone who contributed to the process but, in particular, we would like to thank the following colleagues and collaborators, past and present.

For support in initiating the Kent workshops that inspired *The Research Funding Toolkit*: Prof. Robert Fraser, Dr Janet Haddock-Fraser, Prof. John Baldock and David Coombe.

For insights into the research funding process provided in their capacity as 'Grants Factory' seminar leaders at the University of Kent: Prof. Paul Allain, Dr Peter Bennett, Jenny Billings, Prof. Jon Williamson, Prof. Elizabeth Mansfield, Prof. Simon Thompson, Prof. Mick Tuite, Prof. David Shemmings, Prof. Peter Taylor-Gooby, Prof. Peter Clarkson and Prof. Dominic Abrams.

To Dr Chloe Gallien, Dr David Wilkinson, Prof. Paul Allain, Gillian Brunt, Dr Frances Guerin, Dr Ruth Blakeley, Dr Nicolas Dumay and Prof. David Shemmings for reading sections of the book in draft and providing invaluable feedback.

To Research Services colleagues at the University of Kent for their support and advice: Lynne Bennett, Jo Stichbury, Dr Carolyn Barker, Karen Allart, Rachel George, the late Carol Moran and Phil Ward from the Research Funding team; Ruth Woodger, Kate Ferguson, James Manning, Juan Vidal and Jane Benstead from the Research Contracts team; Jenny Rafferty, Jon King, Jody Turner, Alicia Barron and Stephen Ford from the Research Finance Team; plus Clair Thrower, Nicole Palmer, Dr Kathy Bennett, Simon Kerridge and Sue Prout.

To the editorial team at Sage – Patrick Brindle, David Hodge, Anna Horvai, Ian Antcliff and Katie Metzler – and all the anonymous reviewers for their encouraging and constructive feedback.

To Dr Aylish Wood, Prof. Paul Allain, Prof. Arthur Samuel, Dr John Roughan, Prof. Donia Scott, Dr Ruth Blakeley, Dr Nicolas Dumay and Prof. Simon Thompson for 'donating' funded applications and allowing us to quote extracts from them.

# INTRODUCTION

*The Research Funding Toolkit* aims to improve the quality of your grant applications and help you obtain funds to support your research.

In order to win funding you need to know three things: the function of research grant applications; how and why grants are awarded; and what helps applications stand out in competition.

The system proposed in this book helps you understand these three things and apply this understanding to your own applications. Each recommended technique exploits the common features of major funding agency decision-making processes and is relevant to all research grant competitions that use expert peer review and grants' committees.

The special characteristics of this decision-making process mean that grant applications need a different approach from other types of academic writing. The following features make the grant-writing task so specific:

- Research grants are speculative investments made in response to project proposals. Your applications must persuade decision makers that your project is a sound investment.
- In any research funding competition, project proposals vary widely in topic, approach and subject area. Your applications must encourage grants' committees to see that your projects are the most worthwhile.
- Funding agencies cannot invest in every high-quality project proposal received. You must give decision makers no reason to reject your applications and never exhaust a good idea in one bid.
- Grants' committees work under pressure and deal with a large volume of proposals at each meeting. Your applications must stand out in this environment.

Applicants usually enter research grant competitions by preparing a written submission to a set template. These submissions are assessed by expert referees and, at the end of the evaluation process, a committee of distinguished members ranks the applications in order. Those at the top of the ranking win the available grants.

Those that do not win grants fail for a variety of reasons, including bad luck. It is often hard to tell whether the grants' committee ranked your rejected application highly or not. Even when the agency sends you referees' reports as feedback, these can be contradictory or confusing. This means that applicants find it hard to learn from their mistakes and do not persevere with strong project ideas.

The emphasis throughout this book is on a pragmatic approach that identifies potential weaknesses and improves your chances. As the advice is rooted in the universal structure of the research funding competition, it remains independent of academic discipline or funding agency.

However, each *Toolkit* user will have different needs, depending on career stage, field of research and prior experience of grant-writing. You can identify your personal starting point by reading the following statements and deciding which ones apply to you. Each chapter contains cross-references to other parts of the book that might interest you.

### My research funding success rate is less than 25 per cent.

You may need better pre-submission feedback, help with structuring your project or advice on how to improve your grant-writing skills. *Chapter 3* shows you how to get effective support and advice as you develop projects while *Chapter 11* explains how to elicit constructive feedback on your draft proposals. *Chapters 7* to *10* deal with how to structure and write your applications.

### It takes me a long time to generate fundable ideas and/or write my research grant applications.

You may need to find a more efficient way of developing your ideas and translating them into fundable project proposals. *Chapter 4* explains how to plan and time your applications efficiently. Meanwhile, *Chapters 7* and *8* focus on the generic properties of funding agency application templates and how to complete them efficiently and effectively.

### I want to start winning larger research grants.

If you have had success with smaller grants, you need to know how to write convincing larger-scale project proposals. *Chapter 1* will help you find out whether your ambitions are realistic and the level of grant you should target. *Chapter 8* helps you understand and complete complex application templates. *Chapter 12* addresses the logistics of creating a convincing and comprehensive project budget while *Chapter 13* provides guidance on preparing large, collaborative project proposals.

### I want to make my first research grant application.

You need to understand the principles of research funding competitions and what level to start at. Use *Chapter 1* to find out what sort of scheme is appropriate for your track record and *Chapter 2* to decide which funding schemes to target. *Chapter 5* explains how funding competitions work and *Chapter 7* provides an overview of funding agency application templates.

**I have made a number of applications but have never won a research grant.**

You need to find out where you might be going wrong. *Chapter 1* will tell you if you are pitching your applications at the wrong level. Meanwhile, *Chapters 5 and 9* explain how research funding competitions work and what information decision makers need from your application. *Chapter 10* will help you develop an appropriate writing style.

**The whole process is so bureaucratic and confusing that I cannot face making applications.**

You need to understand the rationale behind these bureaucratic demands and know how to get help in meeting them. *Chapter 3* explains who can help with different aspects of the application process. *Chapters 7* and *8* help you understand the generic properties of application templates. You should also use *Chapters 5 and 6* to understand the funding process from the perspective of the funding agency and your employer.

**My research does not seem to fit the format required by funding agency application templates.**

You need to understand how to structure your projects in a way that makes funding agencies understand their value and confident of their likely success. In order to create highly-ranked applications from your research ideas, you need to understand how funding agencies work (*Chapter 5*), how to structure a research project convincingly (*Chapter 7*) and the requirements of funding agency templates (*Chapter 8*).

**It is my job to help people make research grant applications.**

You will find most of this book useful, depending on the types of researcher you support. *Appendix 1* shows how to put the advice in this book into practice at an institutional level. *Chapters 3 and 7* deal with the importance of obtaining support and feedback while preparing research grant applications.

Each chapter contains a selection of examples, tests or Tools. The Tools are practical exercises that you can use to gain insight into your field, identify funding opportunities, plan your application strategy or develop grant-writing techniques in the context of a particular application.

TOOL 1:    CV BUILDER
How to present your research achievements

TOOL 2:    DEFEND YOUR CORNER
How to predict the perceived weaknesses and misunderstandings that might arise when your proposal is assessed

TOOL 3:    THE FUNDING FINDER
How to generate a list of relevant funding opportunities

TOOL 4:    THE ISOLATION RISK ASSESSMENT
How to find out if you risk becoming isolated within a wider research community

TOOL 5:    WHERE TO TURN FOR HELP
Who can help with each aspect of application development

TOOL 6:    EXPANDING YOUR FUNDING SUPPORT NETWORK
How to create links with other researchers and colleagues who can help you

TOOL 7:    READING REVIEWS
How to read between the lines of feedback on rejected applications

TOOL 8:    APPLICATION TIMELINE
How plan and time your applications in stages

TOOL 9:    BUILDING BLOCKS OF AN APPLICATION
Which grant-writing tasks to tackle first

TOOL 10:   WHAT THEY WANT TO HEAR
How to find information on the funding agency's evaluation criteria

TOOL 11:   WHOSE PROJECT IS THIS?
The role of your institution in managing and taking responsibility for funded research projects

TOOL 12:   WHAT DO WE NEED TO KNOW?
How to generate research sub-questions

TOOL 13:   PRODUCE YOUR EVIDENCE
How to generate and collate the evidence that supports your four key propositions

TOOL 14:   ARGUMENTS AND EVIDENCE: THE 10 STEP PROCESS
A step-by-step guide to constructing an effective application document

TOOL 15:   IS IT WORTH IT?
How to check whether the funding agency's eligible research costs suit your project

TOOL 16:   INTELLIGENT QUESTIONS ABOUT FINANCE
Good questions to ask while planning your budget

THE RESEARCH FUNDING TOOLKIT

# ONE

## HOW TO BE A FUNDABLE RESEARCHER

## Summary

This chapter helps you decide the best approach to winning grants, based on your research interests and career stage. It also helps you assess how your research might rank in the eyes of referees and grants' committee members who will decide whether your projects deserve funding.

There are two Tools in this chapter. The *CV Builder* Tool helps you identify aspects of your career that strengthen your position as a credible research grant applicant. The *Defend Your Corner* Tool can be used to help achieve perspective on your research field and understand how other academics might rate your work.

## Introduction

Chasing research grants can be dispiriting and time consuming. Rejection letters are an almost inevitable part of a research career. With this in mind, you must ensure three things before you start writing research grant applications:

1   You are a credible applicant for the grant you request. This means showing that you have the capabilities needed for every component of your proposed project.
2   You ask a research question that the funding agency will want to have answered.
3   You propose an organised programme of research activities that will answer the question.

The stark truth is that success rates for most grant schemes are often much less than 20 per cent and that writing a research grant application is extremely laborious. There is no point in submitting applications where there is no chance of winning the grant, however well crafted the proposal.

Your first grant-writing task is to find out how attractive you, your research area and your proposed projects are to funding agencies and their decision makers. This process has four elements:

- Are you eligible to apply?
- Is your research field easy to fund?
- Are you a credible applicant for your target funding scheme?
- Will your research topics and methods excite funding agency decision makers?

This chapter takes you through each of these to help you spot challenges that affect your chances of success.

## Eligibility requirements

Rules governing whether individuals are permitted to apply for specific schemes vary significantly between funding agencies. Technical problems mean that you can waste time preparing applications that never make it past the agency's secretariat.

If you are a permanent employee of a recognised higher education or research institution and have residency and a home address in the country in which you are employed, you will find one or more funding schemes for which you are eligible. However, schemes vary widely in their eligibility criteria and you must be aware of the following:

| | |
|---|---|
| Employer | While a higher education or recognised research institution is acceptable to the vast majority of funding agencies, some schemes require the project leader to be from the third sector, health service or industry. If you are an independent researcher you may find your options severely limited and you may need to find an eligible organisation willing to host your project or hire you. |
| Employment status | Funding agencies generally require applicants to hold a formal contract or affiliation with the host institution that extends beyond the end date of the proposed project. |
| Residency | Many schemes make residency (or proposed residency) in a particular country or countries a basic requirement for eligibility. |
| Geography | Some funding agencies and schemes limit applicants to a particular geographical region. |
| Career stage | This is typically expressed in years from PhD. Be aware that 'early career' can mean anything from one to twelve years from PhD. |
| Collaboration | Schemes may be confined to research teams of a specified minimum size or may require the involvement of non-academic partners. |

The first example in this book illustrates the varying eligibility criteria of different funding agencies.

EXAMPLE 1

## THE ELIGIBLE RESEARCHER

Here is an example of how eligibility criteria may vary using three funding agencies that support similar fields in the same country. The Arts and Humanities Research Council (AHRC), the British Academy (the UK's national academy for the humanities and social sciences) and the Leverhulme Trust (a charitable trust supporting research and education) are three of the main sources of research grants for humanities' disciplines in the UK.

This table summarises some of the main differences in general eligibility criteria:

| Funding Agency | Applicant Residency Requirements | Applicant Employment Status |
|---|---|---|
| AHRC | UK residency | Employment (or equivalent) by recognised UK HE institution or research organisation. This must be in place from point of application until three months after proposed end date of grant. Contract researchers whose posts are fully funded by a research grant are ineligible.[1] |
| Leverhulme Trust | Not specified | Employment by a university, HE, FE institution or registered charity in the UK (and, in some cases, developing countries). The minimum employment contract must be for the duration of the proposed project. Contract researchers and retired academics who retain close links with their institution are both eligible to apply.[2] |
| British Academy | UK residency (for most schemes) | None specified for schemes that do not include overheads (full economic costing).[3] |

NB. This information is indicative and prospective applicants should always check the current criteria for the relevant scheme before preparing an application. For more detail on how to find this sort of information about your target funding agencies, please refer to Appendix 2.

Check funding agency guidelines carefully before assuming you can apply to a particular scheme. If you do not seem to meet the criteria, check your status directly with the funding agency and your employer before writing your application. You should also check whether you meet your employer's own eligibility criteria.

---

[1] www.ahrc.ac.uk/FundingOpportunities/Documents/Research%20Funding%20Guide.pdf (last accessed 20 October 2011)
[2] www.leverhulme.ac.uk/funding/RPG/eligibility.cfm (last accessed 20 October 2011)
[3] www.britac.ac.uk/funding/general-info.cfm (last accessed 20 October 2011)

# Your research field

Your key task as an eligible research grant applicant is to convince funding agency decision makers that your question is worth paying to have answered. In brief, all funding agencies want to invest in research projects that ask important questions.

However, what makes a question important varies according to funding agency. Each has its own set of criteria. The agency's website always features these prominently and it is foolish to start writing applications without referring to this information.

The task of choosing which applications best fit these criteria is carried out by a grants' committee, using reports written by expert referees. It is essential to understand some key points about these two groups before you start writing:

- The grants' committee is formed of members whose expertise covers a broad area of the agency's remit, although this may be uneven. There may be no representative of your field or discipline and not all of the members are necessarily academics.
- 'Expert' is a relative term when applied to peer review. A common assumption is that 'expert' peer review means that referees have a complete and detailed understanding of the methods proposed and a boundless enthusiasm for the research question. In practice, they will know something about the field in question but they may not specialise in it.

Consequently, your proposed project may find no natural advocate as it goes through the funding agency assessment process. This is why your applications must create excitement and enthusiasm among non-partisan readers.

To this end, applicants have an advantage if they have a fair idea about possible referees or the likely composition of a grants' committee. Some funding agencies even publish lists of committee members. Others have standing panels with a stable membership. In most cases you can get some information on the type of people likely to review your application or represent it at a committee meeting.

The next example shows how different funding agencies assign disciplines to individual grants' committees.

━━━━━━━━━━ EXAMPLE 2 ━━━━━━━━━━

## INSIDE THE GRANTS' COMMITTEE

This case study illustrates the variety of grants' committee structures and memberships. Using the life sciences as an example, the table below lists some funding agencies that UK-based researchers may target.

| Funding Agency | Grants' Committee Structure and Membership |
|---|---|
| Wellcome Trust | Nine bio-medical discipline-specific *Expert Review Groups* with about 10 members each.[4] |
| Leverhulme Trust | The *Leverhulme Trust Board* consists of up to 10 members, all of whom are, or have been, closely involved in the senior management of Unilever. The board makes the final decision on all applications from any discipline.[5] |
| European Research Council | There are nine *Life Science Panels* out of 25 panels (across all disciplines). Each is composed of 10–15 distinguished researchers acting as independent experts in the subject area of the panel.[6] |
| BBSRC | Four non-clinical life science *Research Committees* with a core membership supplemented by a *Pool of Experts*. About 20 members at each committee meeting.[7] |

The Wellcome Trust is a global charitable foundation supporting biomedical research and the medical humanities. The Leverhulme Trust is a charitable trust supporting research and education across most disciplines. The European Research Council (ERC) is a European funding body that supports investigator-driven frontier research across all disciplines. The Biotechnology and Biological Sciences Research Council (BBSRC) is the UK research council for the biosciences.

This table is a good example of the varying breadth and levels of expertise offered within individual grants' committees that cover the same area. In this case, your application may come before a lay panel that covers all disciplines (the Leverhulme Trust) or a subject specific panel (e.g. 'animal disease, health and welfare' at the BBSRC). In either case, the likelihood of any committee member's interests exactly matching your area of expertise is low. Moreover, direct collaborators will be expected to declare a conflict of interest and play no part in assessing your application.

For more detail on how to find this information about your target funding agencies, please refer to Appendix 2.

In brief, 'fundable' research fields are those that generate projects that excite decision makers from outside your immediate area. The implication for your research grant applications is that you must think and write about your research in a way that appeals to non-specialists.

[4]www.wellcome.ac.uk/Funding/Biomedical-science/Application-information/Committees/index.htm (last accessed 20 October 2011)
[5]www.leverhulme.ac.uk/about/board.cfm (last accessed 20 October 2011)
[6]http://erc.europa.eu/index.cfm?fuseaction=page.display&topicID=66 (last accessed 20 October 2011)
[7]www.bbsrc.ac.uk/organisation/structures/committees/committees-index.aspx (last accessed 20 October 2011)

# Your track record

Every time you make a research funding application, you effectively put a price on your proposed research project and invite the funding agency to pay it. Furthermore, the agency has to pay this price 'up front', before the proposed research project gets underway.

As well as deciding whether the project is value for money, decision makers must be confident that you have the capabilities to carry it out. Unlike academic journals, funding agencies take a calculated and specific financial risk each time they award a research grant. They must also be sure that you will deliver the project you propose.

The most important source of information on your capabilities is your personal track record. Evidence of your previous research performance helps the grants' committee and the referees predict whether you are capable of delivering the proposed programme of research and its outputs. In simple terms, if you have done it before, they will trust you to do it again. If you haven't done it before, then you will have to convince them that you have the ability to do it for the first time.

## Track record and funding scheme

The more money you request, the higher the bar will be set as regards your track record. This is partly because a research grant is a speculative investment. Quite simply, the bigger the investment, the more evidence is needed that you can deliver an adequate return. In addition, bigger projects have more components and you need to show that you are competent to carry out each of them.

Consequently, a small travel grant of a few hundred pounds may be within the reach of a researcher with modest publications. In contrast, a five-year programme grant is only accessible to applicants with impressive publications and who have successfully completed substantial funded projects.

Publications are the principal means by which applicants are expected to demonstrate their track record. They are the expected outputs of successful research activity. If your research has not resulted in publications, this may cast doubt on your ability to complete research projects successfully. In this case, a question mark will remain over whether you can deliver a return on the speculative investment you request.

In general, you or your research team should have published on all of the different kinds of research activity and using all of the research techniques used in your proposed research programme.

If you want to find out whether your publication record is suitable for a particular scheme, just go to the funding agency's website and access the list of previous grant holders. Then go to the personal web pages of the grant holders themselves and check out their publications. You can also consult the funding agency secretariat. If you do not compare well with 'the competition', set your sights lower until you have produced more or higher impact publications.

This seems like a 'catch 22' situation. However, there are ways to improve your publication track record and 'fundability' before making any grant applications on your own. These include:

- Unfunded projects that lead to publication
- Internal research grants from your institution that produce publishable outcomes
- Conference presentations
- Volunteering to help senior researchers or mentors with their projects in return for acknowledgement or co-authorship
- Acting as Co-Investigator on a colleague's research grant

## Track record and project design

Whatever level of funding scheme you target, your applications need to advertise your potential as a grant holder.

It may help your case if referees and grants' committee members already know and respect your work. However, it is more likely that they will be from outside your immediate field. You cannot assume that they know you are competent to conduct the proposed project.

Consequently, make sure that evidence of your achievements is clearly communicated in each grant application. Depending on the funding scheme and your field, give the following information in your application:

- Publications (some funding agencies expect impact factor and citations to be listed)
- Previous or current research grants
- Project management experience
- Esteem indicators (editorial positions, invited talks, relevant prizes)
- Relevant experience in practice, user or knowledge transfer settings
- Evidence of any specialist skills that are not implicit in your publications

Research grant competition success rates are so low that one query about your capability or experience can spoil your chances of a grant. It is safest to assume that referees and committee members are not aware of your research competence. This assumption makes sure you provide all the evidence on your ability to lead a funded project.

## Track record and project scale

The accepted 'entry level' for research project grants varies dramatically according to discipline. If laboratories, equipment and post-doctoral research assistance are the typical resources used for research in your field, a three-year project grant is the usual starting point for first-time applicants. Anything less than that may look a little insubstantial.

However, if your discipline is characterised by collaborative research, you may have the opportunity to act as Co-Investigator (Co-I) on a very large project grant at an early stage in your career. If you work in a field where grant-funded research teams are a rarity, acting as a Principal Investigator (PI) on a one-year project grant may be the normal first step.

At the other end of the scale, travel grants or short fellowships are significant achievements in fields dominated by 'lone scholars' conducting desk research.

In addition, a number of funding agencies offer dedicated 'first grant' schemes for early career researchers and these vary in scale and ambition. Despite the implicit promise of an easier ride for inexperienced applicants, it is worth getting information from the agency about the number of applications they typically get and the number of awards they expect to make. If the number of awards is strictly limited, the 'first grant' scheme may prove more competitive than the equivalent 'standard' grant option.

You can be fairly certain that it is unwise to apply for a five-year 'large' or 'programme' award as your first grant. In order to have a good chance at this level, you must demonstrate successful completion of at least one standard project grant.

In summary, the prerequisite for standard research grants is a publication record that demonstrates a level of research independence and shows that you can deliver every component that makes up the project. If your CV also includes some of the following, this may further strengthen your case:

- Previous employment as a post-doctoral research associate (PDRA) on a prestigious funded project
- Successful completion of a smaller funded project as Principal Investigator
- Involvement on a larger grant as Co-Investigator
- A funded postdoctoral research fellowship

In every case, you are more likely to get funded if you convince the funding agency that you have the skills and capabilities to deliver the proposed project.

# Your topics and methods

If your chosen project is in a field that is not well understood by 'outsiders', do not assume that a well-written application will enable you to buck the trend. Decide whether your field has not yet won funding because it is new and exciting, or because it fails to interest anyone outside it. The cold truth is that it is almost certainly easier to move to a different part of the funding landscape than to rearrange the landscape itself.

It is sometimes hard to look outside your academic silo and get a clear view of whether your field attracts much interest or support from a wider research community. However, there are warning signs that indicate a rocky path to research funding success. These include:

- Marginal interest in your area from your other researchers in your wider discipline
- Lack of interest and confidence in your methodological approach from the dominant branch of your discipline
- Ethical controversy
- Tendency towards hyper-criticism within your field
- Ideological disputes within your field
- Lack of public pressure or political will to address particular health or social issues

Issues such as these can serve to split your discipline into opposing camps or turn your own research area into a sleepy backwater. Neither situation makes it easy to win research funding.

In these situations, it is especially important to realise that excellence and theoretical rigour alone are not enough to win a grant. You also need to generate active enthusiasm and excitement among the decision makers. In order to do this, you must learn how to write grant applications that leave the reader wanting to support your bid.

# Conclusion

This chapter dealt with the factors that make an applicant, research field and project more or less fundable. After reading it, you should be more aware of the main challenges you face to winning research grants and what you can do to present yourself as a credible applicant or to improve your research fundability.

The two following Tools are intended to help you achieve these aims. The *CV Builder* will help you present your research achievements convincingly. *Defend Your Corner* aims to help you analyse your research area in order to identify how funding agency decision makers might react to your research projects.

# CV BUILDER

This Tool helps you to build a CV that will demonstrate your ability to deliver the project proposed in your research grant application.

The CV you attach to a research grant application is rather different from the one used when applying for a new job. For a start, you will often be confined to a couple of sides of A4. Secondly, you do not need to include anything irrelevant to your capacity to carry out the components of the proposed project. As will become clear later in this book, your CV is not the only part of the research grant application where you communicate and reinforce your track record, but it is an important element.

The version you submit for an individual project will show that you can deliver all the project components described in your case for support. Once you have produced an initial project design, make a list of the skills and experience needed by the Principal Investigator and any collaborators.

These might include:

- Proof of ability to produce important knowledge in a relevant area
- Publishing high-impact papers
- Line managing staff
- Supervising research students
- Delivering projects to deadlines
- Relevant data collection and analysis techniques
- Other research skills (languages, IT, dealing with vulnerable groups, etc.)
- Developing networks and contacts (gaining access to sample populations, facilities or archives)
- Organising events (conferences, workshops, etc.)
- Dealing with non-academic groups (e.g. the media, industry, policy makers etc.)

If you make this list of components at an early stage it helps you design your project more effectively. Any glaring omissions in your skills or experience might lead you to consider redesigning the project or bringing in Co-Investigators, project partners and other resources that will help make your project look more convincing.

The next step is writing a CV showing the necessary skills and experience required for your role in the project. Check whether the funding agency gives specific guidance. The sort of information needed includes:

- Qualifications: PhD, other professional training
- Brief employment history: post held, dates, job title
- Previous funding: funding agency, title, dates and value of grant

- (Selected) publications: some agencies want to see impact factor and citation counts as well
- Other dissemination: conference presentations, invited talks
- Relevant training, e.g. media training, specialist research skills training
- Supervision of research students
- Relevant non-academic work experience, e.g. with user communities, as a practitioner, in industry, with the media, outreach work
- Project management experience: include any budget management, event organisation or line management experience that might be relevant
- Other key impact and esteem indicators

You can almost certainly leave off details of your secondary education, your personal details and your teaching or administrative responsibilities (unless directly relevant to the application).

---

TOOL 2

## DEFEND YOUR CORNER

Researchers who are deeply immersed in their field can find it hard to remember that other academics (let alone non-academics) may think their work marginal, incomprehensible or unsound. The Tool will help you identify where you might struggle in your efforts to convince funding agency decision makers that your project deserves a research grant.

According to your personal preference, use lists, diagrams, mind maps or flow charts to create your 'map'. As this exercise deals with your blind spots, it may be helpful to pair up with a colleague and work together to produce one each. Include the following:

| Relevant Research Fields | Notes |
| --- | --- |
| Your research topic | The question you answer in your proposed project |
| Your overall subject area | Use part of the title of the relevant funding panel or take the nearest fit from the list of disciplines provided by the funding agency in its application form |
| Your branch of subject area | How you would describe your research area to academic colleagues from the same faculty |

*(Continued)*

| Relevant Research Fields | Notes |
|---|---|
| The *dominant* branch of your subject area | See which areas of your subject area are best represented on the target funding agency panel or among the college of peer reviewers. Also think about which branch receives the most research grants, most media attention or the highest impact factor for its peer-reviewed journals |
| Any other fields that address similar issues | Be sure to include those fields that are methodologically or ideologically opposed to your own |
| Your methodological approach | How you answer your research questions |
| The *dominant* methodological approach of your overall subject area | How others answer research questions |
| The *dominant* methodological approach of any *dominant* branch identified | How others answer research questions |
| The *dominant* methodological approach of other fields that address similar issues | How others answer research questions |

In respect to both the dominant branch of your own discipline and any other fields that address similar issues, ask the following questions:

| Do other researchers in these fields... | Your Branch | Dominant Branch | Other Fields |
|---|---|---|---|
| Use the same approach as me? | | | |
| Understand the approach I use? | | | |
| Respect the approach I use? | | | |
| Think my topic is important? | | | |
| Cite my publications? | | | |
| Have major ideological differences in choice of topic or approach? | | | |

The yes/no answers to these questions will tell you which sections of your research grant application require additional evidence in order to defend your choice of topic or approach and convince non-partisan decision makers from related fields. If this exercise generated lots of 'no' answers, the field is probably highly specialised. This means you have to make extra efforts to ensure that your research questions appeal to referees and grants' committees and that your methods are well justified.

# TWO

## HOW TO FIND FUNDING

## Summary

This chapter is designed to help you identify the funding agencies that cover your field of research, make the right decisions about which ones to target and pitch your applications at the right level.

The *Funding Finder* Tool at the end of the chapter helps identify suitable funding agencies for your field and gives an overview of how widely funded your area of research is.

## Introduction

There are hundreds of research funding agencies worldwide, many offering multiple schemes. One of your early tasks is identifying all possible sources of funding for your current employment situation, career stage and research interests. In order to target your applications efficiently, you must then understand which agencies offer the most desirable or achievable research grants. In this chapter, we look at identifying relevant funding opportunities and how to decide whether they meet your needs.

In order to create a funding scheme hit list, it is helpful to start by asking yourself a deceptively simple question: why do you want to win research funding?

## Your motives

The reasons why academics engage in the time-consuming and chancy business of making research grant applications can be complex. At a basic level, funded research may be the best or only way of getting the resources or time that allow you to answer important research questions. This is certainly the basis on which the grants themselves are awarded.

However, the academic world is very complicated and applicants often have other reasons for writing grant applications. In practice, these secondary factors often provide an important impetus to seeking research funding.

Even in fields characterised by inherently expensive research, researchers may find themselves subject to one of the following additional pressures. These include:

- Responsibility for a team of research staff who need to keep their jobs
- Heavy teaching or administrative responsibilities that make teaching buy out a very attractive option
- The career-enhancing aspect of a big research grant, especially if research funding success is a condition of promotion or the applicant is planning to move jobs
- Many institutions own large pieces of equipment that can support large numbers of research projects but that also need multiple, concurrent research grants to pay for their upkeep
- Pressure by your employer to bring in income to the institution (see Chapter 6 for further discussion of this)

The reasons listed above are not always of interest to the funding agencies and if these secondary motives shine through your application, your chances of winning a grant may be reduced. However, if these factors are important, you should keep them in mind as you decide which funding agency or scheme to target.

These 'alternative' motives are particularly evident in disciplines where research is desk-based and typically conducted by a lone scholar. In these cases, world-class publications are not dependent on research assistance, equipment or travel. Consequently, applicants of this type must perform a careful balancing act between their motives for applying and the agency's motives for awarding research grants.

In summary, you should always plan applications with a clear idea of why you want research grants. Funding agencies and schemes vary dramatically in the research expenses they offer and the procedures that applications must go through before a decision is made. Success rates are also extremely variable. This means that a suitable-looking grant may not help you to achieve your full range of objectives unless you look closely at the small print before applying.

In brief, there are four categories of worthwhile research grants:

1   Elite research grants

This type of grant often uses a fellowship format and allows you to become a full-time researcher for an extended period. The best are very prestigious and give significant discretionary research and travel funds or full-cost project funding. They are awarded as much on the basis of your talent, previous achievements and potential as on the project you propose.

### 2 Full-cost project and programme grants

As research grants are increasingly hard to obtain, there is no question that a CV featuring a list of substantial funded projects looks extremely impressive. When it comes to promotion and moving jobs, academics with a strong funding track record stand out against colleagues with equivalent publications but no external funding. The most prestigious funding agencies tend to be the highly competitive national and international funding schemes that are not confined to a single discipline.

These schemes all operate a rigorous peer review system and award larger grants within their portfolio of schemes. National, state-funded research councils, learned societies and dedicated research funding charities are prime examples of this category. They offer comprehensive funding for the project that often includes some form of overhead. In addition, they rank highly in terms of academic prestige.

Success rates may be low but winning this category of research grant consistently will mark you out as a successful researcher and valuable member of your academic department.

### 3 Partial-cost research grants

This sort of incidental or partial funding tends to cover activities such as conference attendance or collecting pilot data. These grants should be considered if they help you produce an important publication that will develop your research career. They will also prove useful if you want to change the direction of your research.

If you are lucky in your research topic, you may find a 'pet' funding agency that can consistently provide you with very useful pots of money. Success rates are often somewhat higher than among the national research councils and the application process may be less bureaucratic with a quicker decision time.

On the other hand, the prestige factor may not be as high. However, the grants may be sufficient for you to conduct research that results in important new knowledge and high impact publications. Consequently, this sort of funding agency may find a worthy place in your portfolio of research funding providers.

You can also use partial-cost grants to help you apply for full direct-cost grants by travelling to collaborate with and learn from researchers who are well funded.

Your own institution may also run internal competitions for small research grants and, if used wisely, these can provide a useful platform for publications and other research outputs that lead you to bigger, external grants.

4  Commissioned research contracts

If your discipline is relevant to the public sector or industry, you may be able to engage in contract research that offers very generous financial terms. This sort of research is often allocated in response to tenders by government departments or evolves organically from an on-going relationship with, for example, a private sector organisation. It tends not to be curiosity-driven, though the topic may coincide happily with your interests.

Where findings must remain confidential and for the exclusive benefit of the original funding organisation, you may even attract grants that bear no relation to your publication outputs.

If this sort of research is within your reach, you will apply a different set of criteria. First, ask whether the knowledge outputs of the project will provide social or economic benefit (or 'impact'). Secondly, research that has no clear academic or user output needs to be sufficiently lucrative to compensate.

The list above outlines the four types of potentially useful research grants. In the course of your career, you may also come across some schemes that help you do none of the above and you may be well advised to avoid them rather than take a 'research grant at all costs' stance.

In practice, a desirable funding scheme ticks a number of boxes. At its best, it will be career-enhancing and financially generous, while facilitating high impact publications.

With all of this in mind, the rest of this chapter will help you work out how to discover the following:

- Which funding agencies cover your field
- What sorts of research activity they fund
- Any practical considerations that may affect your choice

## How to identify the relevant funding agencies

The volume of available funding schemes does not mean that you and your research activity are eligible or suitable for more than a few of them. It is more usual to feel frustrated by the limited range of suitable schemes than overwhelmed by your options. However, identifying those funding schemes that are appropriate for your specific field is not necessarily straightforward.

If you work in an organisation with supportive, research-active colleagues and a helpful Research Office, you may have the solution to part of this problem already. Colleagues will simply hand you a list of the funding agencies applicable to your field of research.

In addition, many research institutions subscribe to research funding databases with search and alert facilities that claim to keep you updated on every relevant opportunity in your field. However, you may find that your search criteria return thousands of funding opportunities or none at all. The additional problem with specialist database searches is that they tend to provide a list of funding schemes that, technically speaking, cover your research area. Whether researchers working in your field or in your country have ever succeeded in winning research grants for their area is another matter. You may even find that a general internet search engine can be as useful as a dedicated database search.

However, databases, internet searches and workplace colleagues will be less helpful if one of the following scenarios applies to you and your research:

- You can apply your methods to particular settings, such as specific medical conditions or geographical locations. In this case, you may find that you can approach specialist funding agencies that may not be accessible to your discipline as a whole.
- You access research funding schemes that are not open to applicants from your host country via international collaborators – as an overseas investigator, project partner or consultant.
- You engage in interdisciplinary research and may have better access to funding agencies through collaborators than directly.

Even if you find that funding databases work for you and you think you are aware of the major funding sources for your field, the *Funding Finder* Tool at the end of this chapter may prove useful. As well as helping you identify any additional funding sources, this analysis gives you an idea of how widely your research area relies on external research funding.

## How to identify the relevant schemes

Despite the number of schemes available, it is surprising how often an applicant has an idea for research activity that fits none of them. While caught up with enthusiasm for a particular topic, it is easy to forget that the funding agency has its own definition of importance and its own set of criteria for the research it invests in.

Consequently, you should take a close look at the specific schemes offered by the funding agencies that cover your field in the country where you work before planning research projects in great detail. This will stop you from heading up research funding blind alleys and may give you some new ideas as to the type of project you might propose.

It is also worth bearing in mind that not all the advertised schemes will be suitable for every applicant. There may be restrictions imposed by discipline, career stage or geographical location. There may be only one call a year for a particular scheme and the assessment process can take months, which means that you may be two years away from starting your proposed project.

The range of schemes on offer from large funding agencies includes the following types of grant:

- Studentships and bursaries
- Travel or conference grants for purposes of dissemination or collaboration
- Small grants to include travel, basic research assistance and other modest expenses
- Collaboration grants to support interaction between two or more specific countries
- Project funding designed to support the full costs of a project on a topic nominated by the applicant
- Project funding designed to support the full costs of a project on a topic nominated by the funding agency
- Fellowship funding
- Conference, seminar or network funding
- Large programme grants (three to five years)
- Interdisciplinary research grants, managed programmes or network funding
- Knowledge transfer schemes and industrial partnerships
- Research funding for practitioners, artists or clinicians who want to develop their academic research potential

The detail of individual schemes will vary widely but all funding agencies expect to fund discrete programmes of activity that meet their criteria and help answer (or generate) the questions that they consider important.

In contrast, you are unlikely to find any research funding agencies that are willing to provide financial support for the following:

- Additional time and resources to finish an almost-completed project
- Funding to support a conference, event or trip planned for the immediate future
- Resources to support activity that a funding agency would not recognise as research outside the context of a larger project (such as stand-alone exhibitions or performances that do not fit a formal practice-as-research model)
- Infrastructure costs (except in clearly specified schemes)
- Help with publication costs for work that is already complete

These are all examples of research activity that need financial support in order to go ahead. However, none of the above will count as a discrete research project that encompasses specific research questions, a plan of investigation and a set of outputs. Most funding schemes only support projects with this comprehensive and self-contained structure.

In addition to checking whether the proposed project is likely to appeal to the funding agency, you must also make sure that the project resources are both eligible and reasonable. Once more, it is the funding agency that calls the shots.

Most funding agencies publish lists of eligible costs on their website (look for a separate tab, the frequently asked questions section or in the funding guidelines document). As ineligible items can include 'basics' such as equipment, research assistance or investigator time and vary widely between both agencies and schemes, you need to make sure of the parameters before you go ahead. See Chapter 12 for more information on this.

## Practical considerations

Once you are aware of why you want research funding, practical considerations take over. Research grant schemes all vary and you must be aware of any limitations before matching a project to a funding agency:

- Overall size of grant available
- Eligible staff costs (Principal Investigator time, Co-Investigators, research assistance, non-academic partners, consultants, overseas partners, administrative support, teaching replacement etc.)
- Eligible non-staff costs (equipment, PCs, travel, consumables and books)
- Overheads (which vary widely)
- Requirements for match funding or institutional commitment

However, financial considerations are not the only practical elements to consider when choosing where to apply. Technicalities such as deadlines, success rates and the bureaucratic demands of the application process will also make some funding agencies more workable than others.

## Deadlines and decision times

These range from open calls with on-going assessment of applications through regular quarterly deadlines to annual schemes and one-off or irregular calls for proposals. Some funding agencies operate two-stage processes that mix the two. In any case, there is no remedy if a simple mistake or network failure means that you miss the deadline by a few hours.

You must note the exact deadline, including time of day and time zone, which can work to or against your advantage.

Once the deadline has passed you wait, often for many months, for the decision. If you are lucky enough to receive funding, there is usually a gap of several more months while the contract is prepared or other paperwork completed and you assemble your project team.

The following example looks at the varying lengths of time that funding agencies take to make a decision on your research grant applications.

---

▬▬▬▬▬▬▬▬▬▬ EXAMPLE 3 ▬▬▬▬▬▬▬▬▬▬

## IT'S DECISION TIME

As an illustration of how long you may have to wait for a decision, here are some examples of the varying decision times offered by a range of major research funding agencies:

| Funding Agency | Type | Average Decision Times |
|---|---|---|
| Australian Research Council | Research Council | 6–9 months[8] |
| British Academy | Learned society | 1–7 months[9] |
| MRC (UK) | Research Council | 6 months[10] |
| NIH (US) | Government agency | 9–10 months[11] |
| Nuffield Foundation (UK) | Charity | 5 months (2-stage application process)[12] |

The five to seven month average means that you must begin working on a typical project grant application at least a year before you want to start the research (and that assumes you will be lucky first time). See Chapter 4 for more information on planning your applications. Funding agencies publish this information and it is essential to your long-term planning process.

For more detail on how to find this sort of information about your target funding agencies, please refer to Appendix 2.

### Bureaucracy

The factor most likely to put you off is the time and effort needed to prepare applications. An application to a large national or international scheme easily

---

[8]www.arc.gov.au/media/important_dates.htm (last accessed 20 October 2011)
[9]www.britac.ac.uk/funding/deadlines.cfm (last accessed 20 October 2011)
[10]www.mrc.ac.uk/Fundingopportunities/Deadlines/index.htm (last accessed 20 October 2011)
[11]http://grants.nih.gov/grants/grants_process.htm (last accessed 20 October 2011)
[12]www.nuffieldfoundation.org/application-timetable (last accessed 20 October 2011)

runs to between 15 and 25 pages of carefully prepared text. This may appear to go way beyond the information that seems necessary.

These apparently 'unnecessary' elements may include:

- An explicit justification of every resource requested
- Discussion of ethical issues for low-risk projects
- An account of the impact that the project will have outside its academic field
- An application form with repetitive or irrelevant sections

On the other hand, the page limit for the case for support itself can seem very restrictive. Including all the necessary information on literature and methodology may seem impossible. Consequently, many research grant applications remain incomplete. Others only come to fruition after many months of dogged effort.

The next example looks at the different types of application template used by a range of funding agencies.

---

EXAMPLE 4

## TIME AND EFFORT

The table below illustrates the different application processes for a range of funding agencies covering the same field.

This example takes four different funding agencies that a UK-based experimental psychologist might target. These are: the ESRC (a government funded research council); the Experimental Psychology Society (a learned society funded by membership subscriptions); the Royal Society (the UK's national academy of science funded by gifts, legacies, an endowment and government grants), and the European Research Council (funded by member states through the European Commission).

The level of bureaucracy varies dramatically according to the size of the grants provided and the accountability of the funding agency. At one end of the scale, the anti-bureaucratic Experimental Psychology Society is only accountable to its membership and offers grants of a few thousand pounds. At the other end, the European Research Council gives grants of over a million euros and is accountable to numerous governments through the European Commission.

These differences are reflected in the amount of information required from each applicant.

|  | EPS[13] | ESRC[14] | Royal Society[15] | ERC[16] |
|---|---|---|---|---|
| Application form | Brief applicant details and checklist | Online application form with at least 17 sections including a budget, some involving several paragraphs of text (e.g. summary, impact, staff duties) | Seven section online application form incorporating a CV section, budget and a full research proposal of around 2,500 characters | 'Part A' online application form incl. extensive biographical and career information on PI and host institution plus abstract |
| Mandatory attachments | 1 1,000 word proposal (no template provided)<br>2 One page CV<br>3 Letter of support from host institution | 1 Case for support (6 pp max with template)<br>2 CV per applicant (2 pp max)<br>3 Pathways to impact plan (2 pp with template)<br>4 List of publications/ bibliography (3 pp)<br>5 Data management plan (3 pp max with template)<br>6 Justification of costs (2 pp) | None | 1 Scientific leadership potential (max 1 page)<br>2 CV (max 2 pp)<br>3 Early achievements track-record (max 2 pp)<br>4 Extended synopsis (max 5 pp)<br>5 The scientific proposal (max 15 pp with template provided)<br>6 PhD Certificate<br>7 Host institution statement |

You should also note the very different requirements and formats of 'application forms'. In these examples, the EPS form can be completed in minutes while the other forms may take days and the Royal Society online 'form' incorporates a full research proposal. For more detail on how to find this sort of information about your target funding agencies, please refer to Appendix 2.

The time you have available will, in practice, dictate which of your planned applications you tackle at any given time. In addition, low success rates also mean that researchers may have to make several time-consuming applications (with lengthy waits for the decision) before one of them gets funded.

[13]www.eps.ac.uk/index.php/grants-and-awards (last accessed 20 October 2011)
[14]www.esrc.ac.uk/ (last accessed 20 October 2011)
[15]http://royalsociety.org/grants/ (last accessed 20 October 2011)
[16]http://erc.europa.eu/ (last accessed 20 October 2011)

## Success rates

Statistically, the result of most research funding applications is likely to be a rejection. Success rates can be less than 20 per cent for prestigious project grant schemes and in single figures for sought-after fellowship grants.

Most funding agencies publish their success rates on their website or in annual reports. However, the exact page can be quite hard to find from the home page. A simple internet search for 'success rates' and the name of the relevant funding agency is usually an efficient way of finding the information you need.

Sometimes you receive feedback on why your proposal was rejected but other funding agencies do not provide this in any form. In either case, you must try again or think again. See Chapter 4 for strategies for dealing with rejection.

It is also possible to find the success rates for particular schemes, either by checking the funding agency's website or by asking the secretariat. Some of these success rates are just a few per cent and so small as to reduce researchers to tears. At this level, there will be many more high-quality applications to the scheme than there are funds available.

When grants' committees are forced to rank equivalent applications in order of priority, tiny incremental differences and luck come into the equation. In order to make it through, you must generally win support from both referees (who read your applications very thoroughly) and from the grants' committee (who speed-read them).

In this highly competitive climate, one ignorant or hyper-critical comment can sink your application. This may lead to rejection but does not mean that your project is worthless. A different set of decision makers could easily place the same application those crucial few rungs higher up the ranking and award you a grant.

In any case, a glance at the success rates is an important part of understanding that the hunt for research funding may be a long process. Experienced applicants know that you must never exhaust your ideas in one attempt and you must maximise your chances with extremely well-crafted applications that are submitted regularly. The later chapters of this book show you how to do both.

# Conclusion

After reading this chapter, you should have a clearer idea about the best research grants for your career stage and how to plan your applications. Once you have identified a list of possible funding agencies, see Appendix 3 for more information on how to use funding agency websites. The following Tool helps you to create a list of available funding opportunities and decide which funding schemes provide the best fit for your research.

# THE FUNDING FINDER

This Tool helps you discover the principal sources of research grants in your field and gives you an idea of how much funding your area attracts.

Use the questions below to make a list of funding agencies that are actively involved in funding research in your area. If you do not know the answers already, you can find this information from the acknowledgements section of any published works or by going to the personal web pages of their authors, where research grants are generally listed.

Was your PhD funded by an external organisation? Y/N

> Was the studentship awarded specifically to your project or part of a general allocation to your institution? Y/N
>
> > *List the funding agency, if external.*

What is the principal research activity on which your PhD was based?

> Was any of this research externally funded? Y/N
>
> > *If so, list the agencies.*

Is the research conducted by your PhD supervisor externally funded? Y/N

> *If so, list the agencies.*

Make a list of up to five close current collaborators and research mentors both in your current country of residence and internationally.

> Does their research receive external funding? Y/N
>
> > *If so, list the agencies.*
>
> Are the funding agencies prominent funders within your current country of residence/ employment? Y/N

Is research you cite or refer to in your own publications externally funded? Y/N

> If so, pick up to five pieces of research that you use heavily.
>
> > *List the agencies that funded this research.*

Was any recently-published work in your field externally funded? Y/N

> *If so, pick up to five pieces of research*
>
> > *List the agencies that funded this research.*

Were the most interesting presentations at a recent conference you attended externally funded? Y/N

If so, pick up to five presentations.

*List the agencies that funded this research.*

Which national research council funds your discipline in the country where you are employed?

Has it funded any projects in your area in the last three years? Y/N

Are there any national or international learned societies or charities that cover your area of research? Y/N

Have they funded any projects in your area in the last three years? Y/N

This exercise is likely to yield one of the five following results:

A   *Mainly 'Yes' answers plus a list of **five or more** funding agencies that all actively support projects in your research area and that all cover your current country of residence. Some of these agencies appear on your list several times.*

Your task is more straightforward if your responses fall into this category. If you come up with a long list of potential funding agencies, then you have the luxury of picking those that best suit your work and where you have the best chance of succeeding. The agencies that appear on the list several times should be your first priority if they offer suitable schemes for your career stage.

B   *Mainly 'Yes' answers plus a list of **four or fewer** potential funding agencies that actively support research in your field and that all cover your current country of residence. One or two of them appear on your list more than once.*

If you only identify a handful of funding agencies, then your approach needs very careful planning. This may involve adapting your projects to suit the available schemes and being very careful about which projects you propose to which agencies and when. As success rates are low, you cannot afford to exhaust your one big idea on one high-risk application.

C   *Mainly 'Yes' answers plus a list of funding agencies that have not funded projects in your current field or do not cover your current country of residence.*

If your answers fall into this category, it may be because you have recently moved country and either your existing network of collaborators is concentrated elsewhere or you work in an area that is higher profile in a different part of the world. You might also generate an irrelevant list if your research has recently shifted away from your original doctoral research and now has stronger links with a new area. In both cases, you need to find the funding mainstream for your new area or new country of residence.

*D   Mainly 'No' answers and research in your field is largely unfunded.*

If research in your area has been largely unfunded, you have two difficult choices to make. First, you need to decide whether you want to win research grants. If you don't, that's OK; you will probably be able to sell this book second-hand. If you do want funding, then you have one further choice to make. You have to decide whether you want to change your research field to one where funding is easy, or whether you want to change the world into one where your field gets funded, in which case you will need to think about direct fundraising, which is beyond the scope of this book. The easier course of action may be to switch to a different research field that has greater access to research funding than yours.

*E   Mainly 'No' answers and the questions seemed inapplicable or difficult to answer.*

If you find the questions difficult to answer, this may be symptomatic of a potentially problematic isolation as a researcher. If you find it hard to find examples of published work on related topics or identify established academics who work along similar lines, you will find it difficult to identify suitable funding opportunities. In this case, you need to work on situating your research in a defined field and finding a community of established academics with whom you can interact. You may also find it helpful to consider whether your research may have different applications or if a collaborative approach might give your work a broader perspective.

# THREE

## HOW TO GET GOOD ADVICE

## Summary

This chapter looks at why you need help from others in order to prepare a strong research grant application. It also discusses the people who are best placed to help you and how to develop effective working relationships with them.

There are three Tools at the end of this chapter. *The Isolation Risk Assessment* aims to help you identify any issues with academic isolation, *Where to Turn for Help* provides direction on who to ask for assistance and *Expanding Your Funding Support Network* suggests ways that you can develop a network of useful and informative associates.

## Introduction

A recurring theme in this book is the idea that research grant applications cannot be produced in isolation. While all applicants cite literature in their case for support, some go no further than this in their engagement with the wider research community. Consequently, applications are prepared with limited understanding of how referees or committee members may react to their proposed project and without the benefit of pre-submission feedback.

By working in isolation, you risk the following:

- Losing touch with the priorities (and biases) of the wider research community. Remember, it is members of this community who will review your grant application and decide whether or not it will be funded. You need to know about them even if you think they are wrong.

- Missing the chance to obtain insider knowledge from referees and grants' committee members, who have direct experience of the ways in which official funding agency procedures work in practice
- Losing the opportunity to gain informal feedback from peers and to correct obvious flaws before submitting your application

The rest of this chapter looks at these risks of isolation in more detail and suggests ways to reduce them and strengthen your position as a research grant applicant.

# Research isolation

Research isolation happens when circumstances prevent you from developing constructive working relationships outside your immediate field. As a result, you suffer from a lack of awareness of what goes on in your wider research community.

If you work in a department that enjoys a high research profile for funded research with good integration between researchers of all levels, you have a head start in making these connections. This advantage is increased if you have worked at several institutions.

Wherever you work, it helps to identify and get to know some or all of the following people:

- Experienced grants' committee members
- Regular referees for research grant applications in your discipline
- Consistently successful grant winners for the scheme you target (three or more grants from the funding agency in question)
- Research administrators with experience of the funding agency and the scheme that you intend to target

It is not a disaster if you do not have the optimum levels of help and support. However, you should make a conscious effort to develop contacts with those who have a wider perspective on the research funding system. This group has additional information and experience that supplements the official guidance provided by funding agencies.

Without the help that they can provide, success is much, much harder. If the groups are not represented within your current institution, you need to connect to external networks.

If your employer does not provide much research funding advice and support, start by looking at the websites of other research institutions. You will often find lists of deadlines, information on making successful applications and funding agency news. There are a number of blogs that deal with research grant issues, and following these can also be very informative.

# Institutional isolation

Another category of professional isolation can be inherent to academic careers. Working patterns, office location and internal politics can make academic life solitary. The competing pressures of teaching and administration also mean that research ends up being conducted on the few, precious occasions when you can shut yourself away for a while.

Unless there is a very active research culture, interacting with immediate colleagues can become a marginal activity. It is easy to get into the habit of generally working alone.

However, preparing high-quality research grant applications is much easier with the help of academic colleagues. The input of administrative staff is also essential for ensuring that an application is procedurally correct and for creating an accurate budget.

You must also engage with senior members of your department or institution at the planning stage of the project. At the very least, they will probably have to provide official approval for your project and that may involve making an additional quality judgement about your application.

In addition, you may want to use the prospect of research grant income to negotiate teaching replacement or particular research facilities. Some funding agencies even require levels of institutional commitment or an element of match-funding from employers. All this will require formal or informal negotiation well in advance of the submission date. See Chapter 6 for more discussion of these issues.

Finally, you are in an unfortunate position if there is no one outside your most immediate circle of colleagues whom you trust and respect. This is because informal peer review is very important. The funding agency evaluation process is intensive and necessarily critical. Any material flaw or lack of clarity in your application leads to rejection. The best people to predict potential problems are colleagues from outside your immediate research area. See Chapter 11 for more information on how to test your application.

This is easier said than done. Academics from different branches of the same discipline can be particularly damning of each other's efforts. Differences in methodological approach or in the relative emphasis on theoretical and applied work can lead to dismissive comments.

In this hostile climate, it is understandable that applicants are reluctant to entrust their applications to those who may well be ignorant about or indifferent to their approach. However, initial indifference and relative ignorance may also be the starting position of the academic who provides the official peer review. Consequently, an informal review conducted under similar conditions will provide particularly useful feedback.

# Justifying research plans to others

The fundamental challenge you face as a research grant applicant is the need to submit your research plans to detailed and critical scrutiny by academics who do not share the assumptions and values of your field. Under these conditions of outsider scrutiny, research that you and your immediate colleagues know to be of great importance could receive lukewarm referee reports and a rejection letter.

In order to avoid this, you must learn to explain and justify your research plans in such a way that people outside your field will understand them and acknowledge their importance.

For many academics, it goes against the grain even to discuss their research plans outside their most immediate circle of collaborators. For some, research is a completely solitary occupation. Even academics working on collaborative projects or using team-based approaches in laboratory settings may have rivalries to contend with or concerns about confidentiality.

A bigger problem comes from proposing a programme of activity on which you are especially, and perhaps uniquely, expert. This expertise will be accepted by colleagues in your immediate research field and the specialist audience for whom you normally write. Among your closer colleagues, you do not have to justify the questions you ask, the methods you use or your ability to carry out important research.

However, research grant applications are judged by a wide community of researchers, who may not know or respect you. This community will be specialists in different fields from you. They will be less expert in your topic than you, and far less willing to accept your expertise than colleagues from within your field. But it is this group of outsiders that will decide whether to award you a grant.

Some funding agencies or particular schemes also use non-academics in the decision-making process and this creates a similar set of challenges. Non-academic panel members understand the funding agency criteria and use their experience to judge whether your application fits them. This means that you have to explain your project and its importance in lay terms.

Therefore, the application process requires you to provide evidence that convinces outsiders of the following four propositions:

1 The *importance* proposition: this proposal asks an important question
2 The *success* proposition: this project is likely to answer the question
3 The *value* proposition: the likely gain from this project is worth the resources requested
4 The *competence* proposition: the applicant and team are competent to carry out the project as described

At the end of the process, these outsiders use the evidence you provide to decide upon the quality of your research proposal. See Chapter 5 for information about how they do this.

Grants are allocated according to a set of criteria that meets the requirements of the funding agency stakeholders. If you do not consider these aspects of the grant evaluation process, it will be hard for you to win research funding.

In order to avoid this frustrating and depressing eventuality, get as much insight as possible into:

- The range of academics asked to make decisions about your type of project
- The conditions under which these decisions are made
- What level of specialist knowledge the decision makers might have
- What assumptions or prejudices this group might hold about your field

Although agency guidance and other published material are essential to research funding success, knowledgeable insiders can provide insights that give you an advantage.

Remember also that there is no point making connections if you pick the wrong people. It may be that the colleagues who are most sympathetic or eager to give advice may have the most limited understanding of the process. You need to know who is well qualified to give you help on relevant aspects of your applications.

# Conclusion

After reading this chapter, you should understand that it is very difficult to win a research grant by working in complete isolation. You must develop networks that will provide you with a broad perspective and maximum intelligence about the decision-making process. This process involves a wide community of academics. Almost all of them will be relatively ignorant about your project because they will be experts in and enthusiasts for fields that are different from yours. This chapter concludes with three Tools that help you to assess whether your networks are fit for purpose and to decide how to develop them.

 TOOL 4

## THE ISOLATION RISK ASSESSMENT

This tool is intended to highlight any potential risk of professional isolation. Read the following statements and see which of them apply to you.

Most research grant applicants will find that one or another of these scenarios applies to their case. It is very rare for any academic to find themselves in a working environment that is completely well integrated, high-profile, well-funded and supportive.

> I work in a field, department or institution that has achieved a world-leading position in a specific field and that does not need research funding to maintain its position.

You are well placed to test your ideas and your proposed methods. However, you may be out of touch with the research funding decision-making process if your working environment does not give you access to grants' committee members, regular referees or consistently successful funding applicants. You also need help from colleagues outside the institution to tell you whether your proposal is written in a way that will be intelligible to a grants' committee of specialists in other disciplines.

> My research field is not well represented within my institution and the local research focus is on other areas.

There may be no one in your institution you can discuss ideas, project design and methods with. As a result, you need an external network to help you develop and test your ideas. However, non-specialist colleagues within your institution are in an excellent position to provide feedback on how clearly you express yourself. You in turn can help them.

> I work within an active group of researchers that is well represented within my department or institution. Our research approach is world-leading but it is not well understood in the broader discipline.

You may not be used to explaining the importance and relevance of your research questions or methods to academic colleagues from your wider discipline. In addition, you may not realise that your terminology and language may be incomprehensible to outsiders. A good way to start improving your communication skills is to create a list of criticisms made against your field by those who do not support it. Keep this list to hand as you write research grant applications and address the criticisms, whether you consider them well founded or not.

> I work in a department that is very fragmented and where research groups retreat into their sub-disciplinary bunkers.

You may all be so busy defending your corner that you fail to develop constructive working relationships with people who could give you useful feedback.

You will be better placed to write for a non-specialist readership if you spend time understanding the assumptions and priorities of other groups.

> I am in a relationship with someone who works in the same field and/or many of my friends are direct collaborators or colleagues.

You may find it hard to judge the relevance or importance of your research to those outside your discipline. In addition, you may not realise that your terminology and language are incomprehensible to outsiders. Your friends are likely to provide misleading (though well-intentioned and supportive) feedback on your applications.

> I have only worked in one institution, where I was also a doctoral student.

You may have a limited pool of collaborators. You may also lose perspective regarding what makes a successful researcher in your field. This may be quite different from what makes a successful researcher in your institution. Consequently, you need to start building relationships with researchers who have no connection with your institution.

> Few of my immediate colleagues understand or value my research.

If your immediate colleagues do not understand or value your research, you may encounter the same problems with referees and grants' committees. If, however, your research is nearer the mainstream for your discipline than that of your colleagues, you may need to develop external networks for informal support and feedback.

> I do not respect or value the research conducted by many of my immediate colleagues.

If you work in a department where most of the other research activity is, in your opinion, of doubtful quality, you need to develop external networks. However, you should also use these colleagues to test your applications as they will offer non-specialist, non-partisan feedback. You may also need to learn to respect what they do.

> I am in a minority in my department in that I want to win research grants to support my research.

You may encounter some resistance to your ambitions from colleagues who feel threatened by the possibility of junior colleagues winning prestigious research grants. In this case, you may have to rely heavily on the support and feedback of your external network. See Chapter 6 for more information.

---

## WHERE TO TURN FOR HELP

The list below shows the types of input you can obtain from other people when preparing a research grant application.

1   Insider intelligence on the particular scheme or funding agency before you apply:
    a   Grants' committee members for that funding agency
    b   Regular referees for that funding agency
    c   Colleagues with consistent success from this funding agency (three or more grants)
    d   Colleagues in your institutional Research Office
    e   Your subject research association

2   Administrative or financial details of the scheme:
    a   Colleagues in your institutional Research Office
    b   Funding agency secretariat

3   What successful applications to this funding agency look like:
    a   Applicants with consistent success from this funding agency (three or more grants)

4   What sort of research activity you can afford to fund on this scheme:
    a   Any consistently successful applicants to the scheme
    b   Research Office/Finance Office colleagues

5   Who the referees and panellists might be:
    a   Funding agency website

6   Obtaining institutional backing for your project and any additional resources:
    a   Research Office
    b   Head of Department
    c   Gatekeepers to particular resources within your institution or partner organisations (e.g. participants, archive materials)

7   Informal peer review:
    a   Colleague from similar but not identical field
    b   Known 'sceptics' about your field or methods

---

## EXPANDING YOUR FUNDING SUPPORT NETWORK

In the previous exercise, we identified seven categories of people who are well qualified to help with selected aspects of an application. Start making lists of individuals you know who fit the following criteria.

- Grants' committee members
- Regular referees
- Colleagues with consistent success from the relevant funding agency (three or more grants)
- Colleagues from a similar but not identical field

If you cannot access the above within your own department, you will need to look elsewhere. Use funding agency websites to identify individuals who fit the relevant description and use the following channels to develop contacts with them.

- Funding agency open days, seminars and presentations
- Academic conferences
- Learned societies and think tanks
- External speakers/invited talks within your department
- Institutional research networking events
- Cross-disciplinary research centres at your institution
- Tea room, common room or other informal social opportunities at your institution (even corridors)
- Peer review college briefing events (try to get yourself nominated)
- Institutional visits by funding agencies
- Events and training offered by your Research Office
- Collaborations and visits to institutions that are more research active in your area
- Your subject body or research association
- Email

# FOUR

## HOW TO PLAN YOUR APPLICATIONS

## Summary

This chapter helps you plan and time your research grant applications. Given low success rates, it discusses the need for multiple high-quality applications that give you the best chance of winning research grants. It also looks at how to allow sufficient time for each application and how to make the process more efficient.

There are three Tools at the end of this chapter. *Reading Reviews* helps interpret feedback following a rejection letter. *Application Timeline* and *Building Blocks of an Application* provide a timeline for a typical application and show the different tasks associated with each stage of preparing a research grant application.

## Introduction

As stressed in earlier chapters, success rates for most schemes are low, and applications to fund important, interesting projects are routinely rejected. While academics may be reasonably confident of finding a journal in which to publish good research, the same cannot be said for the funding of good projects.

First, the number of publication opportunities is much higher than the number of research funding opportunities. Secondly, publishing a journal involves less direct financial risk. In accepting a manuscript, a publisher takes on a known quantity and makes a limited financial investment in providing a readership for the research findings.

In contrast, funding agencies make large-scale and speculative investments in a hypothetical project. They are accountable to their stakeholders for their decisions.

They must make thorough assessments of all applications in order to fund projects of the highest quality and with the greatest likelihood of success. However, a large proportion of the applications received will be of similar quality.

Consequently, a grants' committee is faced with the unenviable task of ranking equivalent applications on the basis of tiny, incremental differences. Although these differences become crucial to the ranking process, whether they are genuinely significant or relevant is doubtful.

Even the strongest applications do not generally come through the review process without some small criticism or query. Unfortunately, these minor points can make all the difference to whether you receive funding when there simply is not enough money to go around.

Inevitably, luck plays some part in how critical your referees are and how seriously their criticisms are taken by the committee members. You may have to make several high-quality applications before one of them is ranked highly enough to win funding.

As a result, you cannot rely on one good idea and one single application if you want a reasonable chance of a research grant. However, coming up with multiple ideas and finding time to make multiple applications is an enormous challenge for a busy academic.

The rest of this chapter looks at how to find ways of making the maximum number of high-quality applications in the most time-efficient way.

## The role of luck

If a grants' committee is faced with 40 applications and has funds enough for eight of them, they need to make some tough decisions. There may be two or three outstanding projects that leap to the top of the ranking. There will also be about 20 flawed or pedestrian applications which do not stand much of a chance. That leaves 17 equally worthwhile projects that have all received positive and encouraging reviews. With funding for just five or six projects, the panel has no option but to rank them.

Whichever funding agency you target, your project is in the hands of your non-partisan referees and committee members. Each project has a unique set of decision makers and your personal combination of referees and committee members will affect how highly your project is ranked. Even if everyone in this decision-making group considers your project fundable, you may end up with a rejection letter. The sheer volume of high-quality applications received by the funding agency means that less significant issues have to be considered in the ranking process.

All this gives your research funding application the status of a complicated lottery ticket. You do not stand a chance unless your track record is appropriate, your research question is compelling, your project is well designed and your application is extremely well prepared and crafted. However, there are always more projects that fit these criteria than there are research grants.

If you follow the advice in this book, you will learn how to submit very strong funding applications that always earn a respectable position in the final committee ranking. However, if you want to increase your chances in the research funding lottery, you must accept that some of your high-quality applications will be rejected.

## The impact of rejection

Handling rejection is one of the hardest lessons that you have to learn as a research grant applicant. When you receive rejection letters, you may feel angry, humiliated or depressed. As the original research idea was probably quite dear to you, the sense of failure can be very sharp.

In this way, the lottery metaphor only extends so far. The average lottery ticket is bought with small change and the ticket holder knows that winning is not a personal achievement. In contrast, a research grant application is the repository of your best ideas. The case for support and other documentation take weeks to prepare and are submitted in hope of acceptance and approval. Career success, as well as the opportunity to create important new knowledge, rests on the outcome.

Consequently, having a research application rejected can be completely devastating. It is hard to pick yourself up and work on the next application in the immediate aftermath of a rejection letter. Yet, success rates being what they are, you will probably need to submit several applications in order to win one research grant. Doing this in the face of regular setbacks is a real challenge.

In order to survive these psychological blows, you need to understand and thoroughly assimilate the role that luck plays in research grant competitions. In order to keep positive enough to make the next application, you will also find it useful to keep hope on your side.

## The importance of hope

A good way of keeping hope on your side is to make sure you never get down to your last idea, application or rejection letter. If you keep some overlap between your research grant applications you need never let yourself get back to square one.

In an ideal world, you ensure that you are always waiting for the outcome of more than one application at a time. This means that you keep a constant possibility of success ahead of you. If the availability of suitable funding opportunities or your workload does not make this feasible, then you must make sure you have your next idea ready formed in your head by the time a decision letter is expected.

Even if you do not manage a rolling cycle of proposals, find the time and energy for regular grant applications of a consistently high quality. In order to do this, you need to know in advance:

- Which funding schemes you want to target and when
- How long it will take you to prepare an application
- How to create economies of scale
- Where to get help
- When to give up on an idea

This will require a planned approach with, at the minimum, a general idea about how often you might make grant applications and how you will fit them in among your other work commitments.

# Planning

As it is unlikely that one high-quality application alone will bring you a research grant, it is important that you do not exhaust your ideas in your first attempt.

A rejected application may be eligible for resubmission to the same funding agency but this process is usually subject to a range of conditions and restrictions. While it can be a very worthwhile route to take in certain circumstances, you cannot rely on this option. Consequently, your ideas need to be flexible enough to allow for parallel and complementary applications.

The demand management mechanisms introduced by some funding agencies make multiple, opportunistic bids an unwise strategy. If you clog up an agency's evaluation process with poor-quality applications and re-submissions, you may be banned from applying in future.

This means that you should try to develop a range of high-quality projects for a variety of funding agencies. Each of these will address your research question in a different way or allow you to ask different questions of the same material or through similar studies.

Even without conscious effort, the generation of multiple projects happens automatically as you develop projects to suit the needs of different schemes. Each funding agency that covers your field will have a unique set of criteria and none will have the same set of eligible costs.

If you can take a broad view of your options at an early stage, you will also start to create efficiencies. Some initial thoughts about the projects you could offer to individual funding agencies will save you from 'wasting' a big idea with the wrong funding agency.

The precise range and quantity of available funding opportunities is critical to the planning of your applications. Start by drawing up a list of target funding schemes. This needs to include a note of deadlines, financial parameters, decision times and what each application process actually involves.

You can then let the deadlines themselves start to dictate the order in which you apply. Where the target schemes have no deadlines, you may prefer to start with either the highest priority or the application that has the most realistic chance of being finished within your time frame. Your other work commitments will influence what you decide here.

Before you start fitting specific ideas to the available opportunities, you also need to be clear about what sort of research the funding agency wants to fund. You already know if your field is eligible for the agency in question, so this investigation should be about the style of project favoured and the outcomes that are particularly valued. Always check the current position before applying as funding agencies do change their requirements and emphases occasionally.

It is crucial that your proposed project asks a research question that the funding agency considers important. The likely outputs must also meet the agency's criteria for awarding research funding.

This may seem like a cynical exercise and there is certainly no point trying to throw together a project purely because it seems 'fundable'. The key issue here is trying to find the best fit between what you want to do and what they want to fund. Submitting projects that simply do not match the funding agency's criteria is a waste of time all round.

At the end of this matching process you should have a list of viable funding opportunities from which you can develop high-quality applications. If your list of options has been seriously curtailed by this process, you may need to think again about the fundability of your current research ideas.

## Timing

Once you have generated your list of opportunities and research questions, you need to consider how long it will take to prepare a really well-designed, well-written application. As a guideline, the average applicant with an average project needs to start work at least six weeks before the deadline. Some applications take much longer.

Remember also that your application is likely to require a series of institutional approvals before submission. This means that your internal deadline may need to be several weeks before the external deadline.

In any case, discuss your intentions with your Research Office and Head of Department. Not only is this professional and courteous, it also gives everyone concerned time to deal with the institutional implications.

However much time you devote to your application, you need to pace yourself. There is no point spending months on the perfect case for support if you then leave three days for your budget, the application form and all the required attachments.

In practice, a number of factors are likely to extend the application process if your application involves them. They include:

- Dealing with large numbers of collaborators
- International collaboration
- Inter-institutional collaboration
- The need to recruit steering groups, organise specific events or generate letters of support
- Complex budgets, which might involve gaining competitive quotes for importing expensive equipment, hiring field workers or other 'non-standard' team members
- Complicated costing methodologies, which are time consuming for your Finance Department or Research Office
- Ensuring specific compliance or governance frameworks are in place
- Negotiating a reduction in your personal teaching and administrative load

For some schemes, even six months will prove insufficient. In the case of very large European funding schemes, extensive consortia must work together on demanding and detailed application documents. This process also requires each partner institution to provide a mass of highly technical back-up material. Successful applicants usually have their network of participants in place and ready to go well before the relevant scheme is even announced.

Occasionally, calls for proposals for large and complex projects are issued with very few weeks' notice and at difficult times of the year, such as December or August. If you are well connected to the appropriate networks, it is possible to get advance notice of such schemes. This allows you to complete certain tasks before the deadline is announced. If you are not so fortunate, it is probably impossible to meet these short deadlines.

Even if you are working on a straightforward application as a single applicant, make sure that you leave enough time for informal peer review feedback and institutional approvals. Every application should be given to colleagues to read and comment on well before the deadline.

Chapter 11 explains how to test your proposal, which helps to avoid obvious flaws in the design and presentation of your project. As the feedback may prompt you to revise the project design and budget, as well as the wording of your application, you must initiate this well in advance of the submission date.

You also need to leave enough time for your administrative colleagues to produce staff costs, calculate overheads, ensure compliance with funding agency regulations or provide institutional authorisation for the final version of your budget and application. It is often impossible to submit applications without evidence of this authorisation. Depending on the complexity of your proposal and the number of other proposals being prepared in the institution, this can take days or even weeks.

It is essential to discuss your proposal with your administrative colleagues as soon as you know the deadline for submission. This allows you to negotiate an internal timetable and allows them to guarantee that you meet the external deadline.

# Efficiency

It is likely that your first ever research grant application will involve tremendous effort as you grapple with online application forms, incomprehensible guidance and other bureaucratic demands.

While your project and research question will vary from application to application, there is no reason why you cannot lift phrases, sentences and paragraphs from one application and use them in another. You will find that certain attachments just need revising and updating once you have your basic template in place.

A grant application is unlike a journal article or book chapter in that it need not be an original piece of writing. Always remember that grant applications are not written for publication. If you work in a highly specialist area and have an effective way of communicating the importance of your research questions, be prepared to re-use that text in several applications.

On the other hand, you should not cut and paste from your research articles and reviews. The writing style is completely different. We will see in Chapter 10 that a grant application must be written in such a way that it communicates the essentials of the research proposal to an impatient speed-reader. Research papers and reviews are usually written in a style that requires careful reading and re-reading.

Copying the approach of successful applications to the same scheme may also help you to streamline your efforts. Refer to recent applications by colleagues who are consistently successful with a particular funding agency. Do not follow their approach or style slavishly. However, the level of detail supplied in each section of the application and the way they approach the more esoteric requirements of the funding agency may help you reach quicker conclusions about the best approach to take.

Finally, make sure you keep electronic copies of each application in an editable form, along with all correspondence from the funding agency. Rejection letters are often thrown away when they contain important information, such as reference codes, that you must quote in future applications.

# Giving up

Low success rates mean that high-quality applications often get rejected. The feedback from the funding agency on rejections is often confusing. Referee and assessor comments are often contradictory or irrelevant. This can often make it even harder for you to work out whether the proposed project and question are worth pursuing.

In the absence of clear feedback, consider giving up on a particular line of research after four or five unsuccessful attempts. If you receive consistently damning feedback, consider more fundamental revisions at an earlier stage.

In brief, there are four types of application that do not win funding and you may have to guess which category yours has fallen into:

1 *Unlucky*: important question, strong design and methods, appropriate resources (including research team)
2 *Flawed*: important question, some problems with the design, methods, resources or presentation
3 *Dull*: not very important question, appropriate design methods and resources
4 *Unfundable*: questions seen as unimportant or serious problems with design, methods or resources

Unfortunately, the 'unlucky' category is likely to be a large one and the scoring systems used by funding agencies demonstrate the need to distinguish among a range of high-quality applications. This is clearly shown in the next example, which looks at the grading systems used by a range of funding agencies.

 **EXAMPLE 5**

## WHAT'S THE SCORE?

This case study illustrates the ways that funding agencies design scoring scales to distinguish between high-quality applications.

The table below shows how a range of competitive funding schemes ask decision makers to score applications. The three agencies chosen are the UK's Engineering and Physical Sciences Research Council (EPSRC), the UK's Economic and Social Research Council (ESRC) and the European Commission's Framework Programme 7 (ECFP7).

| Score | EPSRC[17] | ESRC[18] | EC FP7[19] |
|---|---|---|---|
| 6 | This is a very strong proposal that fully meets all assessment criteria | The proposal is outstanding in terms of its potential scientific merit | N/A |
| 5 | This is a strong proposal that broadly meets all assessment criteria | The proposal is excellent in terms of its potential scientific merit | Excellent. The proposal successfully addresses all relevant aspects of the criterion in question. Any shortcomings are minor |
| 4 | This is a good proposal that meets all assessment criteria but with minor weaknesses | The proposal is important as it has considerable potential merit | Very good. The proposal addresses the criterion very well, although certain improvements are still possible |
| 3 | This proposal meets all assessment criteria but with clear weaknesses | The proposal has significant potential scientific merit but is not of a consistently high quality | Good. The proposal addresses the criterion well, although improvements would be necessary |
| 2 | This proposal does not meet one or more of the assessment criteria | The proposal will add to understanding and is worthy of support, but is of lesser quality or urgency than more highly rated proposals. Such proposals are unlikely to have a significant influence on the development of the research area | Fair. While the proposal broadly addresses the criterion, there are significant weaknesses |
| 1 | This proposal is scientifically or technically flawed | The proposal is flawed in its scientific approach, or is repetitious of other work, or otherwise judged not worth pursuing; or which, though possibly having sound objectives, appears seriously defective in its methodology | Poor. The criterion is addressed in an inadequate manner, or there are serious inherent weaknesses |
| 0 | N/A | Not able to assess | The proposal fails to address the criterion under examination or cannot be judged due to missing or incomplete information |

[17]www.epsrc.ac.uk/SiteCollectionDocuments/form-notes/rf-firstgrant.pdf (last accessed 20 October 2011)
[18]www.esrc.ac.uk/_images/ESRC%20reviewer%20scoring%20scales_tcm8-14629.pdf (last accessed 20 October 2011)
[19]ftp.cordis.europa.eu/pub/fp7/docs/fp7-evrules_en.pdf (last accessed 20 October 2011)

Note that the top three scores are all reserved for good proposals with only minor weaknesses. Only proposals in the top category are certain to win a grant. Those in the third category are unlikely to succeed, even though the assessment is positive.

The volume of high-quality applications means that the qualitative differences between applications at the top end of the scale will be quite small. Success is often dependent on fine-grained assessments made by decision makers whose expertise is in other areas.

For more detail on how to find this sort of information about your target funding agencies, please refer to Appendix 2.

Using the guidance in this book should help you produce applications that either win grants or fall into the 'unlucky' category. You only need to give up on an idea when it becomes clear that funding agency decision makers do not consider your question important or have insufficient confidence in your methods.

Of course, whether your research question is inherently unimportant and your research methods are inherently flawed is not the question. What you need to find out is whether the decision makers consider them to be so.

The following Tool is designed to help you understand and interpret funding agency feedback where this is provided.

▬▬▬▬▬▬▬▬▬▬ TOOL 7 ▬▬▬▬▬▬▬▬▬▬

## READING REVIEWS

If you have received a string of rejection letters for a range of high-quality applications on a specific topic, you need to know where you are going wrong. Plain bad luck is still a possibility. However, if any of the following things are true, you can probably improve your luck by revising the application:

- Internal peer review comments: are there any consistent criticisms or any particular criticisms that you have consistently dismissed?
  - o Did the referees fail to understand the importance of the project?
  - o Did the referees fail to grasp exactly what you proposed to do?
  - o Did the referees fail to understand how your research will answer the question you pose?
- Referee and committee member reports (where available). Look for any patterns or consistency on the following crucial elements of your application:
  - o Do the decision makers ever explicitly describe your research topic as important?
  - o Do they ever mention your standing in the field?
  - o Do they ever seem unsure about how you will conduct the project or suggest that your methods are inadequate for the question?

Whether you agree with the opinions of the referees or not, if they fail to appreciate the merits of your proposal you need to improve it. It may well be that the real reason for their negative comments is stupidity or bias. However, that is not their problem. It is yours. The only way you can overcome it is to describe your project with such simplicity and clarity that they understand it, and in such a convincing way that it overcomes their bias. If your project cannot be described in this way, then you need a new project.

# Conclusion

After reading this chapter, you should be aware of how much time and effort making one research grant application involves. You should also have a clear idea about how a planned approach to the process will help create efficiencies and increase your chances of winning a grant.

The following two Tools help you undertake this planning by showing how long a typical application will take and the order in which key tasks should be tackled.

================================ TOOL 8 ================================

## APPLICATION TIMELINE

This chart provides a sample timeline for standard research grant applications. In practice, applicants are often over-optimistic about the amount of time it takes to write a fundable bid.

This timeline is intended to show the different tasks common to most applications and gives an indicative time allocation for each element. The schedule below shows that a six-week preparation period is not too long

| Days until Deadline | Activity | |
| --- | --- | --- |
| | *Collaborative Project* | *Single Applicant Project* |
| 56 | PI checks feasibility of project, starts design, literature review and alerts Research Office and colleagues to the application plan | |
| 51 | PI opens discussions with partners | PI checks feasibility of project, starts design, literature review and alerts Research Office and colleagues to the application plan |

| Days until Deadline | Activity | |
|---|---|---|
| | Collaborative Project | Single Applicant Project |
| 37 | All partners agree to participate and start writing application document | |
| 36 | | PI starts writing application document |
| 32 | Initial draft/plan circulated to partners for input | |
| 32 | Each partner starts preparing budget with Research or Finance colleagues | |
| 28 | | PI starts preparing budget with Research or Finance colleagues |
| 25 | First draft produced | |
| 21–18 | Complete draft and budget produced | |
| 18 | Draft submitted for informal peer review | |
| 14 | Informal peer review recommendations received | |
| 14–7 | Final revisions made to application document | |
| 7 | Final draft submitted for internal approval | |
| 2 | Final corrections made | |
| 2 | Any required letters of support or references received | |
| 1 | Submit application (to avoid technical failures) | |
| 0 | DEADLINE | |

TOOL 9

## BUILDING BLOCKS OF AN APPLICATION

Another way of looking at the workload is by considering the different components of the application template. Some funding agencies prescribe what you include, where you include each category of information and how long each section must be. Other funding agencies offer no template and just specify the number of pages.

However limited the available word count, some of these sections will require considerable planning or fact finding. Realising that you must track down a colleague for key information comes as a nasty surprise when the deadline is hours away.

The list below is not comprehensive but does show the different components of an application and the order in which to write them. Projects often end up at the lower end of grants' committee rankings because the applicant included insufficient information rather than because the question is insignificant or the design is flawed.

| Core Elements | Format | When to Write |
|---|---|---|
| Abstract/summary/ introduction to case for support | A few hundred words that you should write at the end of the whole process and with great care | 3rd stage |
| Objectives | A list of bullet points that explain what you expect to achieve by the end of the project | 3rd stage |
| Research question and/or hypotheses | The question that your investigation will answer. This is usually supplemented by a short list of hypotheses or sub-questions that each relate to a phase or element of the study | 1st stage |
| Background/ literature | A concise, introductory section to your case for support that provides evidence that the question is important and introduces the sub-questions, hypotheses or phases of the research project | 2nd stage |
| Plan of investigation | The main section of your case for support that provides a detailed account of your research methods and analysis in a way that shows how you will answer the question | 1st stage |
| Dissemination | How you will communicate project findings | 1st stage |
| CV | A list of the relevant achievements of a member of the research team. The collection of CVs of the research team must provide evidence that the research team is competent to conduct the project (see Chapter 1) | 2nd stage |
| Budget | A list of all the costs associated with the project, calculated and broken down according to the funding agency regulations | 1st stage |
| Justification of budget | A summary of why each resource is necessary | 3rd stage |
| Non-academic dissemination | Identification of user groups and non-academic beneficiaries and what you will do to involve them and communicate your findings | 1st stage |
| Bibliography | A list of the publications cited in the grant application | 3rd stage |
| Timetable | Graph, table or GANTT chart showing what happens when during the project | 3rd stage |
| Appendices | Technical or legal requirements and attachments | 3rd stage |
| Ethics/compliance | Evidence to show the project will be conducted to accepted standards | 2nd stage |

# FIVE

## HOW FUNDING AGENCIES MAKE DECISIONS

## Summary

This chapter explains how most funding agencies assess research grant applications and decide which ones to fund. It describes the four stages of a typical evaluation process and discusses the requirements that a research grant application must meet in order to succeed in each stage. Chapters 8 to 11 discuss how to write applications that meet all of the requirements.

The *What They Want to Hear* Tool at this end of this chapter helps you find information on how a particular funding agency evaluates applications.

## Introduction

Funding agencies usually try to achieve two different kinds of aims when they fund grants. First, they want to invest in the best research, which means considering the importance of the question and the quality of the project.

Secondly, they support the agency's aims in funding research in the first place. These aims vary according to the status of the agency, its stakeholders and where its funds come from.

Some funding agencies expect all grant applications to address all their aims. However, it is also common for agencies to have a range of schemes that emphasise different subsets of their aims. The application process may be tailored to emphasise the aims of the relevant scheme. For example, capacity building is often supported by specific schemes for Fellowships, which often include extra elements, such as interviews.

In order to meet these various aims fairly and efficiently, agencies develop complex systems for evaluating and ranking the many high-quality applications received. This system is used by most major funding agencies and has specific implications for the way that you design and present your project proposals.

This chapter describes this process, which consists of four stages.

## Stage 1: Application template

You carry out the first stage by fitting your original research idea to the funding agency's application template. The template demands particular types of information in a particular order. It also asks you to replicate, summarise or expand very similar information in a number of places across the template.

Used well, the template helps you to advance a powerful argument in favour of your application and to reinforce it several times. Used blindly, the template weakens your argument and dissipates its force.

## Stage 2: Referees' reports

A copy of your application is sent to each of a number of researchers with expertise in its topic or methods. These 'expert referees' are asked to summarise and to evaluate your application. Depending on the funding agency, you may be offered a chance to respond to referees' reports before the next stage. Some agencies reject grants that get low scores from the referees without sending them to the next stage.

## Stage 3: Designated member presentations

Your application and the referees' reports are sent to members of the grants' committee a few weeks before they meet. A grants' committee may receive over 100 applications for each meeting.

At the grants' committee meeting, one (or more commonly two) of the members give a short verbal presentation on the merits of your proposed research project. The presentation sets out what you propose to do and assesses its feasibility and its importance, and usually ends with comments on the referees' reports and a recommendation to the committee about its score.

The presenters, like all committee members, are researchers, but they may not know much about your field. They probably spend between 30 minutes and two hours reading your proposal and preparing their presentation. They probably make presentations on several applications at the same meeting. They always use the referees' reports to help understand and assess your application.

## Stage 4: Committee discussion

Taking this presentation as a starting point, the grants' committee has a brief discussion about your project. Most committee members have read no more than the short project summary. The committee scores your project. Once all the applications have been scored independently, these are compared and a ranked list is discussed. At this stage, three things happen.

- Grants in special priority areas (such as applications from junior, previously unfunded investigators) may be given a small boost to their score to help them rise up the rankings.
- Minor adjustments may be made to the ranking if there is a consensus that the ranking based on the scores does not correctly represent the relative merits of the application as discussed. 'We all said X's proposal was very high quality but we seem to have scored it just below Y's, which was rather dull.'
- The committee may discuss how much money they have available and how many grants this will fund and where in the ranked list the cut-off is likely to fall.

Each stage of this four-stage process presents threats and opportunities. The rest of this chapter discusses how the assessment process works in more detail. It describes the properties that a grant application must have if it is to resist the threats and exploit the opportunities inherent in each stage of the assessment process.

# Why funding agencies give grants

The application process is designed to fulfil the aims of the funding agency. It allows them to make a decision on the basis of whether funding your grant application is likely to fulfil their aims in a cost-efficient way.

The first aim of funding agencies is usually to invest in the best research. At the simplest level, this requires them to consider whether the grant application offers a realistic promise of an answer to an important question. In order to decide upon this point, decision makers must judge whether your application makes and justifies four key propositions:

1  The *importance* proposition: this proposal asks an important question.
2  The *success* proposition: this project is likely to answer the question.
3  The *value* proposition: the likely gain from this project is worth the resources requested.
3  The *competence* proposition: the applicant and team are competent to carry out the project as described.

In addition, you may identify further propositions that relate to funding agency criteria or the nature of your research. For example, you may also need to convince decision makers that your institution will provide an appropriate research environment. Alternatively, the way that you disseminate results to non-academic audiences may be crucial.

The guidance for applicants provides the criteria used to test how well your proposed project justifies these propositions. Meanwhile, the application template is designed to help you present the relevant information. The guidelines for referees and grants' committees, which may be in the public domain, dictate how that information is assessed.

The way that a funding agency translates the four key propositions into specific evaluation criteria is dictated by the overall mission of the organisation, the fundamental reason why it funds research. A funding agency mission tends to include variable mix of the following four broad aims:

## 1 Health, economic or social benefit

The UK government's main justification for investing in academic research derives principally from the health, economic and social benefits that flow from the projects it supports. It is not alone in this. Agencies funded by other governments and a vast number of organisations, often with charitable status, exist to fund research that provides direct health, economic or social benefits.

While projects are scrutinised for their scientific excellence, theoretical significance is of secondary importance to the potential practical outcomes. Decision makers need to be sure that all funded projects meet the mission of the funding agency and applications must clearly demonstrate how their research serves this purpose. Dissemination activity, user engagement and practical outcomes are of particular importance.

## 2 Promoting scientific excellence in a particular range of disciplines in a particular geographical area

National research councils, funded by central government, usually have this type of remit. They are likely to cover a broad subject base. Applications from different fields, using different paradigms, will be judged alongside each other. In order to succeed, applicants must propose projects that have resonance outside their immediate discipline. In addition, to be successful an application will need to explain its importance in non-specialist language.

## 3 Advancement of a discipline or field

Learned societies and academies that exist to promote a particular subject area or group of subject areas will often include 'advancement of the discipline' in their remit. Many of these organisations provide small grants, which are funded by membership fees and subscriptions. Applicants can be more confident that referees and committee members will apply within-discipline criteria. However, researchers who occupy the fringe of their discipline or work in less fashionable areas may have less chance of success.

## 4 Building research capacity

Any funding agency that includes strong training elements or offers schemes such as fellowships and studentships is interested in research capacity. Decision makers must be sure that awarding the grant helps build the research base in a particular geographical area (such as the European Union) or discipline (such as biomedical science). If you apply for one of these schemes, you must show how you do this beyond the published outputs of the project.

The application process ensures that you include information that allows the funding agency to judge your work against a specific set of criteria. These are designed to allow judgements based on both the primary aim of research quality and the broader set of secondary aims described above.

Each funding agency and scheme has its own idea of what makes research 'important'. Consequently, the way you make and justify your four key propositions changes according to the funding agency you target.

In order to understand the agency's own criteria, read all the guidance fully and include:

- Homepage and 'About Us' sections of the agency website
- Guidance for applicants for the specific scheme
- Guidance for peer reviewers and evaluation templates, if published
- Scoring and weighting systems, if published

The guidance may be articulated in slightly different ways throughout the website and the evaluation template and scoring system will give you some insight into the relative importance of different criteria.

Ask yourself the following questions:

- What makes a project 'important' or 'significant' to this funding agency and scheme?
- Which criteria have most importance?
- Is every criterion formally assessed or are some used as 'tie breakers'?
- Does a project have to score highly against each criterion or are some 'either/or' options?

The next example helps you understand the impact that a funding agency's individual criteria should have on the way you develop potential projects and write your application documents.

EXAMPLE 6

## AGENCY-SPECIFIC CRITERIA

The following lists of key words and phrases are taken from the websites of three major funding agencies. It is clear that, while a researcher may be eligible to apply to all three agencies, the type of research that the three agencies support is very different.

### Leverhulme Trust (charitable trust, all disciplines, UK and developing countries)[20]

Outstanding personal talent – compelling ability – personal vision – wider cultural well-being – surmounting the barriers between the traditional disciplines – work involving notable challenge – significance – excite those working at some distance from the immediate subject area – ability to judge and take appropriate risk – one individual's vision or aspiration – refreshing departure from established working patterns – curiosity – personal development

### National Institutes of Health (government agency, public health, US and international)[21]

High scientific calibre – relevant to public health needs – address the scientific mission of the NIH – significance – important problem – effect – adequately developed, well integrated, well reasoned, and appropriate – original and innovative – investigators appropriately trained and well suited – scientific environment – institutional support – protection from research risk – inclusion of women, minorities and children

### European Research Council (European Commission funding agency, all disciplines, open to member states)[22]

Intellectual capacity and creativity of Principal Investigator (PI) – ground-breaking achievements and publications – establishment or consolidation of independence – commitment to project – ground-breaking nature and potential impact of the research – important challenges at the frontiers of the field – ambitious objectives – possibility of a major breakthrough with an impact beyond a specific research domain/discipline – feasible

---

[20]www.leverhulme.ac.uk (last accessed 20 October 2011)
[21]http://grants.nih.gov/grants/grant_basics.htm (last accessed 20 October 2011)
[22]http://erc.europa.eu/index.cfm?fuseaction=page.display&topicID=498#fields (last accessed 20 October 2011)

---

For more detail on how to find this sort of information about your target funding agencies, please refer to Appendix 2.

The evaluation process ensures that decision makers apply the right criteria. Consequently, it is essential that every research grant application you submit exploits the opportunities and avoids the threats posed by the four stages. The first stage involves fitting your grant application to the funding agency's application template.

## Stage 1: Application template

In order to provide a level playing field and promote efficient decision making, funding agencies must ensure that:

- All applicants provide the required information
- All applicants provide the same quantity of information
- Referees and committee members can identify each category of information quickly

This is usually achieved by standardising the document in which you write your grant application. In practice, this means that you often have to fill in a lot of forms and follow a set template for each element of the proposal.

If the agency receives its funding from government sources, the application documents are more likely to be long and complex. In contrast, a charity may expect applicants to describe a large project with an elaborate design in a few paragraphs, especially if it operates an outline application stage. Either template presents considerable challenges. Failure to respond appropriately to these challenges is the first 'threat' posed by the template.

You may find that fitting your project into the required format is very frustrating. Failure to overcome this frustration could be fatal. You may think that the template demands a great deal of information about irrelevancies while giving you insufficient space to describe crucial aspects of the project. Chapter 8 and Appendix 2 provide help and advice on how to understand different template formats and complete them efficiently.

Application templates are designed to get the information the funding agency decision makers need. Your frustration is a sign that either you find it difficult to give them information that they need or you want to give them information that they do not need. This is the first and most important threat posed by the application template. Failure to give them what they need will lose you the grant. Insistence on giving them information they don't need is also likely to be damaging.

Scrutiny by the funding agency secretariat is the first hurdle that your application must cross. The secretariat will check that each grant application:

- Meets funding agency and scheme eligibility criteria
- Contains all the required components in the required format
- Is reviewed and assessed according to set procedures

After submission, this group will check your application and return it if it fails to meet the required format.

Just fitting your project to the funding agency template is a considerable task for many applicants. In the struggle to meet word counts, justify costs and produce all the necessary annexes, it is easy to forget that the grant application document also has a job to do. It must communicate the four key propositions of *importance*, *success*, *competence* and *value*.

You must also communicate, by direct and indirect means, that your project meets the explicit and implicit criteria for the relevant funding agency.

Moreover, this communication has to be done in a way that suits the working conditions and expertise of the decision makers. The advantage of the application template is that, used properly, it gives the opportunity to communicate exactly what you need to in exactly the way that is best for the evaluation process.

## Stage 2: Referees' reports

A number of 'expert referees' will be asked to provide independent reports on your application. Your second challenge is to ensure that your application document impresses these individuals and helps them to score it highly against the funding agency criteria.

In order to do this, you must understand more about the likely abilities and limitations of the expert referees. In brief, you should never take 'expert' to mean that referees are particularly knowledgeable about your individual research area or sympathetic to it.

## Choosing referees

Potential referees are chosen in a number of ways. Common routes include a standing Peer Review College, academics cited in your project proposal or your own direct nominations. Regardless of the method by which they are chosen, there are some general truths about referees that you should bear in mind:

1 Referees can be hard to recruit and the people who accept the job of refereeing your proposal may not be the most appropriate for your project.
2 Even appropriate experts may not be sympathetic to your approach or methods.
3 Over-enthusiastic and highly sympathetic referees may well be taken less seriously.
4 Referees' identities are protected. This protection is designed to allow them freedom to express opinions that may be unpopular with the reader (you). It may make them

feel that they can unleash petty rivalries that are normally kept in check. There are two aspects to this:

- ○ Colleagues that praise your work 'to your face' may express a different view of it under the protection of anonymity.
- ○ The funding agency will discount reports that appear to be excessively negative or motivated by spite.

## What referees do

The referees will provide a detailed evaluation of your application and grade it according to a particular set of criteria. They are not generally paid to do this and are given a limited period of time in which to do it.

Their motives for agreeing to undertake peer review may include personal career development or curiosity about what is going on in their field.

Whatever their reasons, reviewing your application may be an unwelcome extra task as the deadline approaches. They will probably want to get through the job as quickly as possible. Consequently, you need to make it easy for them to do a good job quickly.

For this reason, your application must be clearly written and easy to read. It must provide enough background material for the outsider and provide evidence that your project meets the funding agency's criteria.

If your application is hard to read or understand, your referees will not be able to do their job easily. If you have failed to include enough information about your research methods, project management, dissemination or why you need particular resources they will be unable to score it highly.

## Peer review criteria

Referees have clear guidance on how to assess your application. They are usually expected to provide their comments and grading on a form provided by the funding agency.

As an applicant, you can often access the referee's form from the funding agency website. Familiarity with the assessment criteria before you start writing helps you to focus on communicating the four propositions.

The peer review criteria vary from agency to agency and from scheme to scheme. However, they usually include some of the following:

- Importance
- Contribution to the agency's declared priorities
- Originality, timeliness and novelty
- Contribution to theory, knowledge or methods

---

- Capability or competence of research team and/or institution
- Appropriateness of design and methods
- Value for money
- Outputs, dissemination
- Likely health, economic or social benefit
- Risk
- Career development and training of project staff
- Project management

If you understand the agency's priorities, you can make sure you highlight how you meet them throughout your application document. In achieving this, the guidance for referees and committee can be as useful and important as the guidance for applicants. The next example shows how this sort of information helps focus your research grant applications.

EXAMPLE 7

## SCHEME-SPECIFIC CRITERIA

This case study illustrates the usefulness of the scheme evaluation form and/or selection criteria while developing an application. This extract from the guidance of an Australian Research Council scheme[23] shows both the evaluation criteria and the weighting given to each item, as follows:

> All Australian Laureate Fellowships Proposals which meet the eligibility criteria will be assessed using the following selection criteria:

> **Investigator (40%)**

> Consideration will be given to the candidate's research opportunities and performance evidence relative to their level of achievement:

> - research output and achievement
> - potential to undertake ground-breaking research
> - outstanding leadership ability
> - potential to leave an enduring legacy
> - contribution to national and international public policy debates and initiatives

> **Project/Program of research activity (30%)**

> *Innovation*

> - are the project aims and concepts original and innovative?
> - will new methods, technologies or theories/ideas be developed?
> - how does the research program enhance innovation in Australia?

---

[23]www.arc.gov.au/ncgp/laureate/laureate_default.htm (last accessed 20 October 2011)

*Approach*

- are the conceptual framework, design, methods and analyses adequately developed, well integrated and appropriate to the aims of the project?

*Significance and national benefit*

- does the research address an important problem?
- how will the anticipated outcomes advance the knowledge base?
- is there a contribution to public policy formulation and debate?
- what is the potential of the research project to result in economic, environmental, social and/or cultural benefits for Australia?
- what is the potential for the research to contribute to the National Research Priorities?
- will this research sustain or enhance international research collaboration?

**Mentoring/Capacity building (30%)**

- potential to build world-class research groups/teams and/or centres over the term of the proposed project
- exceptional ability to supervise postdoctoral researchers and other early-mid career researchers
- record of successful postgraduate supervision, where applicable
- exceptional leadership and organisational ability to ensure the development of scale and focus in research
- ability to attract financial resources to enhance research capacity

If your target scheme publishes specific evaluation criteria in this detail, you can ensure that your application contains evidence that allows a high score against each of these points. For more detail on how to find this sort of information about your target funding agencies, please refer to Appendix 2 and see Chapter 9 for more information on how to generate the right arguments and evidence.

## Stage 3: Designated Member presentations

The final decision on whether or not to fund your grant application will be made by the grants' committee.

Some funding agencies have highly specialist grants' committees, devoted to a single discipline. Other funding agencies have no disciplinary remit and grants' committees with predominantly lay memberships. Consequently, it is useful to understand the composition of the relevant committee before your submit your application. However, in general:

- Committee members are unlikely to be specialists in your subject
- Committee members will have very little time to prepare for their meeting
- Each committee meeting may deal with over 100 applications

## How the committee operates

Most committees cope with the lack of time and expertise by using a 'Designated Member' system. Each application is assigned to two committee members, whose task is to understand it and present it to the rest of the committee, along with a recommended score and a summary of the referees' reports.

Although attempts are made to give applications to committee members whose research overlaps with the proposed project, this is not always possible. You cannot assume that anyone on the committee will have a good understanding of your research area.

In any case, each committee member absorbs an enormous amount of specialist information in advance of the meeting. The Designated Member who presents your grant to the committee may also present many others. In order to succeed at this stage, your application document must:

- Be easy to read, especially to 'speed-read'
- Be easy for a non-specialist to remember, understand and summarise (this helps the designated committee members prepare his or her verbal presentation about your project)
- Make it easy for readers to reconstruct the essence of your proposal and communicate how it meets the four key propositions to a group of non-specialists
- Provide an 'at a glance' overview of your project for the rest of the committee

## Stage 4: The grants' committee discussion and ranking

After each presentation there is a brief discussion. The application receives an overall score. When all the applications have been scored, they are ranked in order of their scores and prepared for a final decision.

There is very little time for in-depth consideration of the relative merits of applications. Each project gets a few minutes of discussion and there is not much opportunity for one committee member to break down the resistance of colleagues and alter the fate of your project.

However, take advantage of the fact that the whole committee will discuss and score your application, even though most of them will only have glanced at it briefly. You must make it possible to get a strong and favourable impression of the logic and organisation of your project from a few hasty glances during the discussion. Your application must be speed-readable.

The jobs of the referees and committee members are rather different. As discussed in the previous section, referees operate as individuals and evaluate your project in isolation. The referee makes a decision about the quality of your application without reference to competing projects. Armed with your application document, a form and some guidance, each referee grades your application and writes a report on it. The referees' reports are sent to the grants' committee with the application documents.

How far the designated members can use their own judgement and override the opinion of referees varies according to the particular funding agency. However, a skilful operator on the committee can undermine even a well-written report from a true expert. At the very least they can discredit the opinion of referees who have done their job poorly.

## Preparing for the committee meeting

Committee members have a tough job both as individuals and as a group. As individuals, they assess a pile of applications with their associated referee's reports and lead discussion of them at the committee meeting. They must have a passing acquaintance with the other applications that come before them and contribute intelligently to the ranking process.

They are less likely than referees to be specialists in your area and have even less time to consider your project. As successful academics, they do not want to look like fools by giving a confused or inaccurate verbal précis of your work and its likely importance. They will also be reluctant to go out on a limb to support you when their colleagues want to trash you. Unlike the referees, they do their part of the job under scrutiny of their peers.

Your application document must give them the evidence they need to make claims in its favour, especially if they wish to challenge the conclusions of the referees. It must also provide the at-a-glance overview that allows every committee member to feel able to comment intelligently about why your project seems important.

The next example demonstrates the essential similarities (and crucial differences) between two research funding agencies' decision-making processes.

EXAMPLE 8

## THE DECISION-MAKING PROCESS

The following table illustrates the way in which grants' committees operate using two specific examples of UK research councils, the Biotechnology and Biosciences Research Council (BBSRC) and the Engineering and Physical Sciences Research Council (EPSRC).

There are significant differences between the two. BBSRC committee members are involved in the initial choice of referees and may discount their assessments. In contrast, EPSRC panel members are not involved in the choice of referees and are explicitly directed not to re-review proposals in the panel meeting.

However, in both cases, committee members have a two-week period in which they must:

- Become familiar enough with their assigned proposals in order to lead a discussion on them
- Prepare to discuss every proposal that comes before the committee
- Contribute to the final ranking of every application that comes before the committee

| | BBSRC[24] | EPSRC[25] |
|---|---|---|
| Allocation of proposals | Each application normally assigned to at least two committee members ('Introducing Members'). Each Introducing Member will usually present between eight and 15 applications at each meeting. | Every proposal is allocated to two speakers responsible for leading a discussion based on the input from expert reviewers. Each panel member is assigned as a speaker for a number of proposals. |
| Choice of 'Designated Members' | Assignments based on scientific expertise and balance of workload. | Assignments align with speakers' expertise if possible. |
| Role of panel | Introducing Members comment on the appropriateness of the referees nominated by the applicant, and suggest additional referees before the peer review process starts. Referees reports are obtained for the assistance of the committee. Although the committee takes into account their comments, they do not form the sole basis for its decisions. | Speakers are not involved in the choice of referees. The panel does not re-review proposals; panel members are appointed to represent the collective views of the expert reviewers and to bring the benefits of their general experience in science and engineering research. |
| Timing | Committee meeting members are sent all the paperwork relating to every application at least two weeks before the meeting. | Panel members are sent all the paperwork relating to every application two weekends before the meeting. |
| Pre-meeting tasks | Introducing Members are asked to send their preliminary assessment to the office in advance of the meeting. | Speakers are asked to send in their initial proposal gradings before the meeting. |

---

[24]www.bbsrc.ac.uk/organisation/structures/committees/committees-index.aspx (last accessed 20 October 2011)
[25]www.epsrc.ac.uk/funding/apprev/panels/Pages/whathappens.aspx (last accessed 20 October 2011)

THE RESEARCH FUNDING TOOLKIT

| | BBSRC[24] | EPSRC[25] |
|---|---|---|
| Role of referee reports in committee meetings | Referees reports are obtained for the assistance of the committee. Although the committee takes into account their comments, they do not form the sole basis for its decisions. | Panels are asked not to re-review proposals but to prioritise proposals through a relative assessment of quality based on the reports of the expert reviewers, taking into account the applicants' responses to the reviewers' comments if provided. |
| Designated Member presentations | At the meeting the Introducing Members give an overview of each assigned application, highlighting its merits and any potential problems. | The first Speaker introduces each proposal, drawing on the reviewers' reports and recommends a grade, taking care not to re-review. The second Speaker comments on any differences of opinion they may have from the first Speaker. |
| Discussion | Discussion is then open to other members who wish to comment. | Other panel members may comment on the proposal and recommended score. |
| Final scoring and ranking | After the discussion, the Chair will agree the overall rank with the committee.

The committee will finalise the ranking, especially those falling close to the likely margin for funding. The final rank order represents the consensus view of the committee taking into account all of the assessment criteria. | At the end, the panel will be asked to agree on the ordering of the proposals, including prioritising those with the same grade and identifying the cut-off point on the list, below which it believes funding would not be appropriate.

The resulting output of the meeting is a rank ordered list. |

For more detail on how to find this sort of information about your target funding agencies, please refer to Appendix 2.

# Conclusion

After reading this chapter, you should know how to succeed in the peer review and committee assessment process by producing application documents that work for a variety of audiences. The secretariat, referees and assessors and other committee members have different roles and read your application in different ways. Each must find the evidence they need that your project is worthy of funding. Chapter 10 of this book will help you write applications that achieve this aim.

The Tool that concludes this chapter helps you identify the official guidance you need in order to write a fundable grant application and understand how your application document will be used during the evaluation process.

---

**TOOL 10**

## WHAT THEY WANT TO HEAR

In order to write a fundable application you need to know as much as possible about who will assess it, under what conditions and using what criteria.

The following information and guidance is usually available from funding agency websites or the secretariat and will be invaluable:

- Funding agency mission statement or description of the sort of research it funds. This should be easily accessed from the home page of its website
- Peer Review College and grants' committee membership lists
- Evaluation and scoring criteria for referees and assessors and/or template forms
- Programme specification document, including full details for application and assessment procedures
- Specific guidance on the content and structure of your case for support, the application form and any annexes

You should familiarise yourself with this information before you start writing. When you have a final draft, use the tests in Chapter 11 to check your application against agency criteria. It is often interesting to realise that the qualities of your project that you think are most important are not those on which it is assessed.

See Appendix 3 for more information on how to find relevant sections of funding agency websites.

---

# SIX

## HOW TO GET THE BEST FROM YOUR EMPLOYER

## Summary

This chapter discusses the three-way relationship between researchers, their employers and funding agencies. It also considers research funding as an institutional revenue stream.

The *Whose Project is This?* Tool at the end of this chapter will help you negotiate this three-way relationship more effectively by showing where your employer is obliged to take responsibility for your funded research projects.

## Introduction

There are at least three partners in a funded research project: the research team, the funding agency and the host institution. In most cases, the host institution is also the main employer of the project team.

The role of the host institution in funded research can cause conflict between employer and researcher. This is unhelpful as a good working relationship between these two parties is essential to the success of your project. For more information on the more complex partnerships that exist within collaborative research projects, please also see Chapter 13.

Three factors influence the potential for problems:

1  As the host institution takes responsibility for the proper conduct of externally funded research, the question of project ownership arises at an early stage in the application process. The power struggles and political issues that ensue can strain the relationship between employer and researcher.

2   Research grant income makes an important contribution to the reputation of an academic institution and can also be a significant part of its overall revenue. This leads to an emphasis on the financial value of funded research that leaves some researchers feeling resentful.

3   In contrast, unfunded or partially funded research is a drain on resources. For some institutions, the benefits of publication provide insufficient return on the expense of providing staff research days, study leave and use of facilities.

These three factors make the research funding process subject to both institutional controls and pressures. As a result, academic staff are often under pressure to win as much funding as possible, particularly from agencies that contribute a high proportion of research costs. Those who succeed often become more powerful within their institution.

This situation creates political issues within institutions. If you do not take steps to resolve them, you may find yourself hampered in your efforts to win grants.

## Who owns your research grants?

Very few research grants are awarded personally to individuals. Although named researchers lead applications and take intellectual ownership, the grant is awarded to a host institution.

In formally accepting a new research grant, the host institution takes legal responsibility for the project. In particular, it declares itself willing to provide the resources specified for the sum of money requested in the application. Once a grant is awarded, the host institution also takes responsibility for the correct financial administration of the grant and any other legal or regulatory requirements.

In brief, your employer owns your grant. If you move to another job during the lifetime of the project you will need its permission (usually given) to transfer the project to your new institution.

Equally, if your project goes wrong, your employer may be held responsible. This will certainly be the case if the problems relate to legislation, ethics, health and safety, human resources or financial management.

This responsibility also extends to compliance with the funding agency's own internal procedures. Major funding agencies conduct audits on host institution compliance. If your employer fails one of these audits, the agency can impose financial penalties or refuse to accept further applications from that institution.

All of the above mean that there are aspects of your applications and funded projects that your employer will keep under tight control. These controls may seem pointless or counterproductive to you. However, you will have very little room for negotiation if you do not try to understand the priorities and concerns of your institution.

# Who wants funded research?

Despite this, the benefits of winning research grants outweigh the risks, as far as your employer is concerned. Research grants are an important revenue stream and source of prestige for many academic institutions.

The reputation of the institution can even rest on its ability to attract research funding. In addition, it will also use research grants as a way of meeting broader objectives, such as increasing the number of PhD students or maintaining research facilities.

Consequently, you may find yourself under pressure from senior management to apply for grants with rewards if you succeed. This may lead to unfunded researchers feeling marginalised. If rewards such as fast-track promotion and lighter teaching loads are reserved for researchers who win grants, these feelings are intensified.

This results in political struggles that make working life uncomfortable for all concerned. Even researchers who want to make grant applications will feel this, especially if they need support or permission from senior 'unfunded' colleagues.

As a result, you may face a series of institutional obstacles in your efforts to make research grant applications:

- Extensive bureaucratic checks to ensure that your proposed project meets institutional, funding agency, legal and regulatory requirements
- Management pressure to apply to more lucrative funding schemes or to include additional resources in your application
- Lack of encouragement or selective encouragement from senior colleagues

# What does your research cost?

Some research grants cover investigator time and a contribution towards institutional overheads as well as all the direct expenses of the project. Others only cover some of these elements or fund them partially. Assuming that you are paid a salary and that your employer provides your office space and equipment, the part of your working day spent on research costs your employer money.

If your employer provides research days and study leave for academic staff, then this cost can be quantified. If your research is unfunded, you are left to show how your publications and other outputs provide sufficient return on this investment.

The rest of this chapter suggests ways to address institutional restrictions, pressures and political problems.

# Restrictions

In authorising your research grant applications, your employer (or other host institution) accepts that:

- It can pay for all the requested resources from the project budget
- The institutional resources that you claim will be available to the project (including your time) will in fact be available to the project
- All proposed activity is legal and ethical and meets relevant governance or regulatory requirements
- The project follows funding agency rules regarding eligible costs and activity

In addition, it will check that the proposed project does not compromise other areas of its activity or overstretch institutional resources. If you win the grant, the host institution signs a contract with the funding agency and guarantees that:

- The funds will be spent as agreed
- The research team will provide reports as requested by the funding agency
- The host institution will monitor and manage the project as required by the funding agency

Some of your institution's concerns and responsibilities may not interest you or seem important to the outcome of your investigation. As an experienced 'host institution', your employer may assume your indifference to these matters. Consequently, it is likely to impose a series of checks and procedures to ensure that funded researchers comply with the necessary rules.

If you take the view that a research grant is entirely 'yours' and that most institutional controls constitute unwarranted interference, you may end up in conflict with your employer. If this happens often enough, you will get a reputation for being difficult.

This means that your research applications will be subject to closer examination before they are approved and that administrative colleagues will be reluctant to help you resolve bureaucratic issues.

It is better to accept that your employer has a legitimate claim over some aspects of your research grant application and cooperate with its requirements. A positive working relationship is more likely to lead to flexibility when you have genuine reason to believe that bureaucracy may harm the research process itself.

The Tool at the end of this chapter highlights those areas where the host organisation has responsibility for your project.

---

# Pressure

Your employer needs to generate sufficient income to cover its expenses, which include your salary. Consequently, it expects a return on the investment it makes in you. If you can show that return in terms that your employer accepts, you will strengthen your position at work.

Understanding how your employer generates its income is essential to this process. In summary, an academic institution may receive its revenue from some or all of the following:

- Student fees, especially any higher fees
- Government grants (based on the numbers or types of students recruited or other factors such as overall research quality)
- Research grants
- Consultancy or enterprise income or sponsorship
- Profits from catering, accommodation and conferences
- Bequests, trusts and donations
- Investments

These sources will vary according to the nature and history of your employer as well as which country you work in. In order to consider your place in this, you must understand which institutional revenue streams your post supports and to what extent.

Depending on the revenue source, your job description and your talents, any of the following might be acceptable answers:

- You attract large numbers of postgraduate or overseas students
- You teach a large number of well-subscribed undergraduate modules, help students achieve high standards and receive excellent feedback
- You are an efficient and effective senior manager who helps your institution run efficiently and cost-effectively
- You win multiple, high-value research grants
- You attract enterprise funding and hold a clutch of patents, from which your institution benefits
- You keep your institution in the public eye by frequent appearances on TV chat shows, writing newspaper columns, presenting documentaries or by providing sound bites for news channels
- You are a world famous expert in your field who drags your institution up the international league tables

If your research is not fully funded by research grant income, you need to show how your research supports other areas of institutional activity. Unquestioning acceptance of individual research priorities is no longer the norm.

Consequently, if colleagues and management do not know who you are or what you do, you may be in trouble. If you use institutional resources for activity that rewards you personally but that your employer does not value, you will also encounter problems.

One of the great advantages of research grants is their direct link between an individual researcher and the institutional balance sheet. This gives funded research higher visibility than shared activities such as teaching and administration. If you win large research grants that include investigator salaries or overheads, you can make a precise account of your financial return to your institution.

In addition, you can argue that the grant and its outputs enhance the research profile of your institution. Finally, external funding means that an institution's internal resources are not depleted in order to support your research.

Consequently, your employer may put you under pressure to make grant applications and provide high recognition and rewards if you succeed. In some cases, this combination of pressure and incentives may prompt you to win grants. If applied clumsily, they can damage the chances of talented individuals or the overall success rate of research groups. For example:

- Managers put applicants under pressure to include additional costs on applications whether relevant to the project or not
- Your department takes a 'democratic' approach with each member given equal opportunity to make applications despite obvious inequalities in their chances of success

As a result, applying the wrong incentives can mean fewer grants rather than more. Equally, if your working environment does not accommodate the demands of application development, the likelihood of success is lower for all.

You and your colleagues may already find it difficult to keep publishing while coping with heavy teaching and administration duties. In this situation, the benefit in making time-consuming and high-risk grant applications may not be obvious.

In summary, institutions can set a disproportionate value on research grant income while failing to support applications in the best way. This has three implications for you if you work under these conditions and want less pressure and more support.

1  You must show that you are a stronger candidate for research grant success than your colleagues.
2  In the absence of incentives, you must find time to make fundable applications.
3  You must show clearly how you succeed in contributing to institutional or departmental goals.

THE RESEARCH FUNDING TOOLKIT

Different sections of this book will help you do these things. See Chapter 1 for advice on how to establish your 'fundability'.

# Politics

If you win lots of research grants (or show the potential for doing so), unfunded colleagues may feel threatened by you. Equally, if you take on high levels of teaching or administration, you may resent 'funded' colleagues and their privileges.

The way that academic institutions operate in practice is often very different from the way that their leaders think they operate. Lack of support for management decisions, personal ambition and fear are just some of the factors that encourage staff to resist, ignore or subvert institutional initiatives.

If funded research attracts particular rewards in your institution, colleagues will find ways of maintaining a status quo that suits their interests. These may include:

- Senior researchers encouraging applications from those who support their interests rather than those with the best chance of success
- Unfunded senior staff blocking applications by keen junior staff
- Research group sub-cultures in which funded research is generally devalued
- A ruthless personal focus on winning grants at the expense of shared responsibilities such as teaching or administration

Enthusiasm and a strong track record may not be much help if any of these scenarios apply to you. In the most toxic cases, you may have to choose between finding yourself another job or getting rid of this book.

However, once you start winning grants the balance of influence may shift in your favour and the barriers may become easier to overcome. The following techniques are useful in navigating your way through political problems:

1 Establish your eligibility to apply for research grants directly with your Research Office. Familiarise yourself with institutional objectives and query departmental objectives that appear to contradict them.
2 Use documented appraisal processes to obtain written agreement on your plans from your line manager.
3 If your line manager blocks your progress, establish supportive relationships with other senior researchers and make your research potential visible to senior management in the wider institution.
4 Ensure you follow all internal procedures to the letter and cannot be prevented from applying because you have failed to give sufficient notice or inform the appropriate colleague about your plans.

5 Choose funding agencies and schemes that do not ask for institutional commitment. Also be careful about fellowship schemes or demands for teaching relief. Acknowledge the problems this might cause colleagues and make constructive suggestions.

6 Use the advice in Chapter 3 to establish independent support networks. Use these to get independent feedback on your draft applications.

7 Accept that your initial set of applications will have to be made unobtrusively and with no impact on your other duties.

# Conclusion

After reading this chapter, you should understand that funded research projects are a three-way relationship between you, the host institution and your target funding agency. This will equip you to deal constructively with any restrictions and pressures that do not seem to suit you or your project. The Tool that concludes this chapter helps you clarify the roles and responsibilities of host institution and applicant.

==================== TOOL 11 ====================

## WHOSE PROJECT IS THIS?

The host institution for a research grant needs to ensure the following:

1 **The project budget is accurately and comprehensive**. This may force you into providing more financial detail and providing more detailed budget breakdowns than you feel are necessary or realistic.

2 **You do not overspend your grant if it is awarded**. Even the best planned budget may not be able to accommodate all possible price rises, salary increases or changes in exchange rates. Nonetheless, the funding agency is unlikely to give you extra money to cover any changes to your costs. For example, some funding agencies do not pay the full cost of inflationary increases to staff salaries. On longer projects you may have to terminate post-doctoral research associate contracts a few weeks earlier than planned.

3 **Unspent funds are returned to the funding agency**. You cannot use the money on other research projects.

4 **The budget is spent correctly (for example, that the staff budget is not diverted into travel)**. The host institution expects you to receive written approval from the funding agency for significant changes in expenditure. The options for diverting funds is strictly limited by funding agencies.

5 **Staff are recruited and paid in accordance with the host institution's policies and procedures**. Generally, you will have to pay standard rates and use your institution's standard contracts of employment and terms and conditions.

6 **The research project conforms to legislation and regulations such as: employment and tax law; health and safety guidelines; data protection; ethical guidelines or formal research governance procedures**. You may not be aware of all the relevant regulations and will probably have to fill in forms with extensive checklists in order to obtain institutional approval.

7 **The project meets funding agency regulations regarding expenditure, management and reporting**. The host institution will also face penalties if you do not comply with these requirements.

# SEVEN

## HOW TO SAY WHAT NEEDS TO BE SAID IN THE CASE FOR SUPPORT

## Summary

This chapter helps you structure and present your funding proposals effectively. It describes a generic structure for your case for support that you can adapt to any funding agency application template. By explaining the function and properties of the case for support, it helps you develop research grant applications that communicate the right information in the right format.

The *What Do We Need to Know?* Tool helps you present your project in a logical and consistent way. In addition, you will find a number of extracts from successful grant applications, which illustrate some of the advice and guidance. You can find more information about each of these in Appendix 3.

## Introduction

Preparing fundable research grant applications is very time consuming and low success rates make the outcome uncertain. Applicants usually have to make several high-quality applications in order to win one grant.

There are two main obstacles to making multiple applications quickly and efficiently:

- Funding agency criteria and templates vary so widely that it is difficult to develop projects or proposals that fit more than one agency
- Each individual application is time consuming as many funding agencies provide a complex application template to complete

This chapter helps streamline this process so that you can take less time to make multiple high-quality applications. It does so by explaining the generic properties of a fundable project and the generic functions of an effective case for support.

Although funding agencies may use different formats for their templates, the information required is usually rather similar. However, these similarities can be hard for a busy researcher to identify.

First, identical section headings can be misleading. 'Introduction', 'Background', 'Track Record' and 'Methods' can mean different things to different funding agencies. Second, different section headings may be used for identical content. 'Summary', 'Project Outline' and 'Abstract' usually mean the same thing.

Reading the funding agency guidance carefully is the only way to understand what the agency requires for each part of its template. However, this chapter also proposes that the diversity of funding agency templates masks many common properties. In brief, differences are often superficial and the underlying structure of application templates remains constant.

Ultimately, a generic approach allows you to create and replicate high-quality research grant applications in less time.

## The 'fundable' project

As discussed in Chapter 5, funding agencies use their evaluation process to collect evidence for four key propositions about your project. These propositions and the evidence that supports them demonstrate whether the proposed research deserves funding:

1  The *importance* proposition: this proposal asks an important question.
2  The *success* proposition: this project is likely to answer the question.
3  The *value* proposition: the likely gain from this project is worth the resources requested.
4  The *competence* proposition: the applicant and team are competent to carry out the project as described.

Although specific evaluation criteria vary widely, they always have these four propositions at their heart. Understanding this will help you develop fundable projects and adapt them to different funding agencies.

## The effective case for support

The research proposal or 'case for support' is the central narrative of your research grant application. This document contains all the essential information about your project and is usually several pages long.

For inexperienced applicants, writing a case for support that interests and convinces busy, non-specialist readers is a daunting task. This document is usually supported by an application form and a set of appendices. The sheer volume and variety of information required can make the whole process confusing and frustrating.

The process will be much clearer if you understand the core functions of a case for support, how it relates to other sections of the application template and how it is used to evaluate your project. There are two main things you need to know:

- The case for support is the heart of an application. Most agencies expect the case for support to contain all the information needed to allow a committee to decide, in principle, whether a project should be supported.
- Other parts of the application template tend to consist of repeated or expanded sections of information included in the case for support. They will also include reference material or information that is only of use to specialist reviewers.

You must also understand the role of the case for support in convincing the referees and grants' committee members who will decide if your application gets funded. There are three things this aspect of your application must do to excite them, to convince them of your four key propositions and stand out against the competition.

- It must get your 'foot in the door' by exciting readers about your research plans and provide a preview of the project
- It must show that 'we have a problem' that needs a research project like yours to solve it
- It must demonstrate that 'this project is the solution' and convince decision makers that they want to fund your project

The rest of this chapter discusses these three functions and provides some illustrative examples of how they work in practice.

## Section 1: A foot in the door

The first thing your case for support must do is to excite readers about your research plans and provide a project overview. Once you have got your 'foot in the door' and engaged your readers' interest, you can move on to detailed information about your research plans.

By previewing the entire project in the first few paragraphs of the case for support, your planned activity is easier for non-specialist readers to understand. This section also prevents detail-readers from losing the overall picture as they tackle the more in-depth sections of the document. Equally, it makes all the headline information about your project available to speed-readers, who may only ever read this section of your application.

The 'foot in the door' element of the case for support is closely related to the 'Summary', 'Abstract' or 'Project Outline' sections of the wider application template. In a two-stage application process, the first stage primarily has a 'foot in the door' function. This section should form no more than 20 per cent of a full case for support and can be as short as one paragraph. It primarily supports the 'importance' and 'success' propositions.

## Objectives

In brief, the 'foot in the door' is the first element of the generic case for support. It is like the salesman who puts a foot in the door to give himself a few precious seconds to describe what he is selling and why you need to buy it. In the context of a grant application, this means:

- Getting readers excited about the project
- Previewing detailed information that you present in later sections of the case for support

Funding agency guidance seldom points out that non-specialist grants' committee members have many high-quality applications to read before they meet. However, you must assume this and write with the intention of making your project stand out against the competition.

The agency often requires a separate project summary that helps get your 'foot in the door' and this is very important. However, applicants must also ensure that the opening lines of their case for support always preview the entire project.

## Serious readers and casual readers

There are two categories of reader to consider here. First, there are the 'serious' readers, who need detailed information about your particular project. Second, there are the more 'casual' readers, who need a basic understanding of every project that comes before the committee.

The serious readers are the referees, the chair of the grants' committee and the members designated to present your proposal to the committee. This group knows that they will have to understand the case for support and explain it to other knowledgeable and critical people.

They want to do this job well and in a way that makes them look and feel good. They will approach your case for support with a feeling of determination tinged with anxiety. They know that they are going to have to understand and explain the case for support. They will want to know how much effort this will take.

They also want to know whether the effort will be repaid. For this, they need a sense that your research problem is important and your programme of research deals with it effectively. Your 'foot in the door' section should make them believe that they have struck lucky.

The casual readers (most of the other committee members) approach your case for support with a more relaxed frame of mind. They have read all the grant applications that they themselves have to present to the committee. They look to see whether your application is interesting enough for them to read and accessible enough for them to contribute to the debate.

Your 'foot in the door' text should convince them that both these things are true. Remember, however, that they do not have much time. Indeed some of them will read your case for support for the first time while the committee is discussing your application. Make it easy for them to get up to speed quickly so that they can contribute to the discussion before it ends.

There are three stages to getting your foot in the door:

- Stage One: Attention and orientation
- Stage Two: Establishing the importance of your question
- Stage Three: Previewing the project

You may find it useful to refer to Appendix 2 as you follow the advice in this chapter. It provides a comprehensive breakdown of application templates, what functions they perform and how they are read and used by different categories of reader.

## Stage One: Attention and orientation

A general principle of grant writing is that you should give the reader the information that they want when they want it. The question of what they want and when they want it is mostly common sense. So, the first thing they want to know is what the project is about.

For serious and casual readers alike, the first sentence of the case for support is crucial. It must be simple and it must tell them what the project is about. This is just as important for highly technical or abstract research as it is for applied projects with obvious benefit.

---
EXAMPLE 9
---

### OPENING LINES

Here is an example of an effective first sentence from a funded application. The applicants begin their case for support with the research question itself:

This project asks how the extraordinary rendition and proxy detention of terror suspects has developed and whether they are US-led phenomena. *Rendition and Detention Project*

Inexperienced grant-writers prefer to start with a slow build-up about their topic that gradually gets to the point and demonstrates their grasp of the field. Alternatively, they start with a quirky quotation from a philosopher or public figure. In doing this, they hope to stimulate the reader's curiosity and demonstrate their own erudition.

Unfortunately, slow build-ups and erudite quotations are bad tactics in grant-writing. Grant-readers are in a hurry. They want to know straight away what your project is about. You should tell them.

---

## Stage Two: Establishing the importance of your question

The next two or three sentences of the 'foot in the door' section put the research topic in context by dealing with its importance.

If the topic is specialist, it may be necessary to explain what developments make it important to study the topic now. If the topic is obviously important, you need to emphasise how your approach to the topic is likely to be fruitful.

You should also take care not to overstate the importance of what you will do. You do not need to pretend that for a few hundred thousand pounds you will succeed in a couple of years where decades of research costing millions of pounds have failed.

At this stage in the case for support, you just need to state why the question is important. This is not the place to bombard the reader with arguments, counter-arguments and citations.

============ EXAMPLE 10 ============

## IMPORTANT QUESTIONS

The following extract from a funded proposal explains why investigating a memory phenomenon called 'reconsolidation' is important:

Most evidence comes from the neuroscience literature, and despite 40 years of animal studies on this phenomenon, it is still strikingly absent from cognitive psychology and psycholinguistic research. There is no reason, however, why humans should be immune to reconsolidation and, in fact, a handful of neurobiological studies on human participants now demonstrate how reconsolidation substantially impacts upon procedural, associative, as well as basic episodic memory. *Memory Research Project*

---

This successful fellowship application appeals to the reader's own experience as a consumer of 'image-making technology' to show how the topic merits investigation.

> Are image-making technologies establishing a language that is altering how we see the world? We know that moving image technologies are rapidly evolving and proliferating. In technologically advanced societies we have become used to moving images conveying ideas and telling stories. But are we aware of the extent to which technological interfaces participate in shaping the language of moving images? *Digital Media Fellowship*

These two examples use different approaches and the differences are worth noting. The first uses simple language to explain a gap in the scientific literature while the other addresses referees and grants' committee members as though they were lay readers (which they often almost are). Both techniques are effective in establishing the importance of the proposed research.

---

## Stage Three: Previewing the project

In Stages One and Two of the 'foot in the door' section you set out your stall by stating your research question and showing why your question is an important one. Your next task is to preview the project itself.

Your readers now understand what your research question is and are willing to accept that it is important. Your final 'foot in the door' task is to mention why your question needs an externally-funded project to answer it and deserves the grant requested.

The most effective way of doing this is to give a brief preview of the project structure and how the proposed components of research activity combine to answer your research question. In order to do this you will need to break the question down. This is also the place to state how the public will benefit from the results of your project.

---

EXAMPLE 11

---

### PROJECT PREVIEW

The following funded application deals with the reduction of pain in laboratory mice. By breaking the question down into three different things 'we urgently need to know', the applicant establishes that a substantial research programme is required now:

Many of these animals develop experimental or spontaneous tumours that are assumed to cause pain so guidelines on assessment and application of humane endpoints have been developed (UKCCCR 1988). These aim to reduce suffering by advising that animals are humanely killed before they experience unacceptably intense pain. However, current guidelines are relatively arbitrary and not based on objective assessments of animal welfare. We urgently need to know:

- If different types of cancer models cause pain?
- At what stage of tumour development pain occurs?
- Which models cause the most pain, and so most compromise welfare?

Answering these questions would allow us to avoid using tumour types that were likely to cause pain and, when this was not possible, to develop better evidence-based guidelines for the application of more humane endpoints. *Research Animal Project*

The next example is taken from the summary of a five-year research project on word recognition and the applicant uses this section to introduce the three themes to be explored. As with the previous example, the project overview is followed immediately by a summary of the benefits of this proposed research programme.

The current proposal includes a large set of theoretically-driven empirical studies of lexical activation. The empirical investigations are organized into three interlocking groups of experiments. One set of studies examines how phonetic variation can affect lexical access, and can even change the lexical representations themselves. Such variation can have surprisingly powerful effects on how words are represented in the lexicon. A second set of studies examines even more fundamental changes in the lexicon: How do adults add new items to their mental lexicons, and what are the consequences of such changes? The third set of experiments investigates the dynamics of lexical competition: How does the activation of one lexical item affect the activation levels of other lexical entries? *Spoken Word Project*

Note that both examples break the project down into several distinct components and show how funding these projects will lead to specific benefits and outcomes.

In summary, remember that the 'foot in the door' section must be written so that it can be read very quickly. Do not try to develop detailed arguments and justifications. Make clear and simple statements. You will have the opportunity to repeat and to justify these statements in the next two sections.

Assuming you have a limit of six pages for your case for support, your 'foot in the door' section should be about one page long. As this section summarises the other two sections of the case for support, you should probably write those sections first.

## Section 2: We have a problem

Your readers already know what your problem is and have a basic understanding of how you intend to solve it from the 'foot in the door' section. Your next task is to provide evidence in support of the 'importance', 'success' and 'competence' propositions (and aspects of the 'value' proposition).

Every funding agency devotes a section of its template to this task and this is part of the template that applicants often misunderstand and misuse. The headings tend to be quite general and with labels such as 'Introduction', 'Background', 'State of the Art', 'Rationale' or 'Timeliness'. These general headings sometimes encourage applicants to include too much irrelevant information.

In brief, the 'we have a problem' section should form no more than 30 per cent of your case for support and focus on supporting the four key propositions.

## Objectives

The function of the 'we have a problem' section is to present evidence from the literature and other published sources that show:

- This problem needs solving (the *importance* proposition)
- You have the skills and experience to solve this problem (the *competence* proposition)
- The proposed project is the best way to solve this problem (the *success* and *value* propositions)

If you cannot provide evidence for all three assertions, the funding agency will reject your application.

## Stage One: The problem needs solving

As an expert in the field, you will be very familiar with the literature and your challenge here is to cite evidence that is pertinent to your 'we have a problem' task. A common mistake is to include too much irrelevant material about the wider field. Applicants often show a virtuoso command of the literature but fail to convince the reader that their particular problem needs solving.

You should present a short list of reasons why the problem needs solving and follow each of them with evidence. These reasons should be realistic. Any excessive claims and hyperbole will make readers doubt the integrity of your arguments.

EXAMPLE 12

## EVIDENCE FOR THE PROBLEM

The first example establishes the need for a new approach to web authoring and does so by explaining the limitations of existing solutions:

> The use of Conceptual Authoring represents a novel approach to Semantic Web interfaces. The advantage of Conceptual Authoring over alternative approaches is that it definitively solves the habitability problem. Users compose texts by choosing from options generated by the system; as a result, the content of the text can never stray outside the system's conceptual repertoire, and no automatic interpretation of text is needed. Evaluation studies have shown that even for complex technical material, the interface can be used effectively by domain experts after only minutes of training [8]. Existing applications have, however, a serious limitation: with one partial exception [11], they are restricted to the editing of assertions (A-box) based on a fixed ontology and fixed linguistic resources. The challenge in the current proposal is to remove this restriction, allowing the same kinds of users to add new concepts and the linguistic patterns for expressing them—thus overcoming the adaptivity barrier as well as the habitability problem. *Web Authoring Project*

In the second example, the applicant explains why the physical presence of the proposed Visiting Fellow will enhance the field of Performance Studies in the UK.

> Schechner is an expert lecturer, a vivid storyteller and teacher, who can distil and communicate complex ideas. Yet even when he shows film extracts of his own work in his lectures, these do not begin to communicate the combined wealth of his practical and theoretical knowledge. Passing on this research knowledge can only be done through practice, through embodied learning and reflection. *Theatre and Performance Visiting Fellowship*

In both cases, it is easy to identify the problems ('habitability' and 'passing on research knowledge') that the projects propose to solve.

### Stage Two: You have the skills and experience to solve this problem

The second stage of 'we have a problem' must establish your capacity to lead the proposed project. Essentially, this means citing your own work and that of any collaborators. In doing so, you should follow three self-citation rules:

- Be honest about the importance of your contribution. The referees will easily spot false claims that your work leads the field when it is merely confirmatory or incremental. This will severely damage the whole of your case for support because it will cast doubts on your competence and professionalism as a researcher.

- Do not only cite your own work, as this may give the impression that you are the only person working in your research area. This will cast doubt on the importance of your research area to the wider world.
- Cite your own work to show your research competence for this specific project. For this reason you might want to cite your confirmatory work with a disclaimer, such as 'We have confirmed this finding', to give the implicit message that you have the necessary research competences while acknowledging that you do not lead the field.

---

EXAMPLE 13

## SELF-CITATION

This is an example of self-citation from an early-career researcher. It establishes the Principal Investigator's innovations in the field, the contribution of other leading researchers and its compatibility with discoveries in related fields:

> Consolidation itself is a fairly new concept in the domain of word acquisition. As my work with Gareth Gaskell has shown, sleep plays a major role in this respect: new words do not integrate our mental dictionary immediately, as a mere function of exposure, but instead require an interval of sleep to do so (Dumay & Gaskell, 2005, 2007, and submitted; Dumay et al., 2004; Gaskell & Dumay, 2003). After sleep, not only the explicit knowledge about the novel words is enhanced (i.e., participants are better at recalling words learnt yesterday than words learnt just before the test), but more strikingly these words now compete with similar sounding existing words for access to consciousness in the course of word recognition (cf. Bowers et al., 2005; Clay et al., 2007; Tamminen et al., 2010, for related findings).
>
> For example, in one experiment, we taught participants new words (such as 'lirmucktoze') and then looked at their ability to detect the embedded existing word (e.g., 'muck'). The expected interference from the newly acquired word emerged only after a sleep interval (Dumay & Gaskell, submitted). In other words, sleep improves—but also integrates—new knowledge with existing information.
>
> Findings like these fit exactly with the idea of a dual learning system (O'Reilly & Norman, 2002; McClelland, McNaughton, & O'Reilly, 1995), in which novel words are initially learnt in the hippocampus and later on interleaved with existing lexical knowledge over a longer period of time as part of their reduplication in the neocortex (Davis & Gaskell, 2009). *Memory Research Project*

This extract establishes the applicant's position in the field while showing that the research topic is of interest to other researchers and fits with findings from related areas.

---

THE RESEARCH FUNDING TOOLKIT

Placing your own contribution in context avoids the common self-citation error of implying that other researchers are barking up the wrong tree and that your approach is the only right one. There are two reasons why you should avoid doing this:

Other researchers in your area are likely to have the opportunity to influence the funding decision by writing referees' reports. If your grant application rubbishes them, they will be tempted to rubbish you in their reports.

A fight within a discipline gives the impression to a grants' committee that the discipline is not making progress. It is far better to praise the work that others in your field have done and point out that their results put you in a position to make further progress. Remember, but do not quote, the famous twelfth-century saying that we see further because we stand on the shoulders of giants.

---

## Stage Three: The proposed project is the best way to solve this problem

There are plenty of important research questions that can be solved without external funding. If decision makers suspect that you could conduct your research without external funding, they will not award you a grant.

In order to agree that solving your problem requires a funded project, the reader needs to understand how each element of research activity helps answer the research question. This means developing your 'foot in the door' preview into a more detailed account of the proposed project structure.

In practice, every fundable research project has more than one component, strand, phase, sub-project or theme. Each of these elements should be linked to a specific sub-question aimed at solving the overall problem.

Inexperienced grant applicants often forget to demonstrate why an externally-funded research project is likely to solve the problem effectively. They focus on expert discussion of the topic that displays their insight into the main issues. Unfortunately, this approach does not explain or justify how the proposed project is likely to solve this problem.

 EXAMPLE 14 

## THE NECESSARY PROJECT

These successful applications establish the need for a funded research project simply and concisely in the 'Background' section of the case for support:

This project asks the following question:

- How has the global system of rendition and proxy detention developed, and how does it operate?
- It will investigate the development and operation of rendition and proxy detention by asking the following three sub-questions:

  1  Is the global system of rendition and proxy detention US-led, or is it a more diffuse system with distinct and partly autonomous regional sub-systems that serve specific local as well as US interests?
  2  Are there any regional differences in the ways in which rendition and proxy detention have developed and are operated?
  3  Can we identify any specific evolutionary moments or shifts in the development and operation of rendition and proxy detention? *Rendition and Detention Project*

In contrast, the following applicant uses the 'Objectives' section of the application template to demonstrate the four things that this research will establish and, therefore, how the project will solve the problem:

The current proposal will more reliably establish:

- The relationship between cancer growth stage (i.e. tumour burden) and pain;
- The occurrence and time of onset of pain in 3 common models of cancer in mice;
- Whether innovative behavioural and pharmacological testing methods can be used to assess the subjective experiences of mice with cancer;
- Whether current endpoint estimates are appropriate and how they can be improved. *Research Animal Project*

In both cases, the scale of the research activity needed becomes apparent as the question is broken into a group of smaller and more specific sub-questions. This process shows referees and grants' committee members that solving the problem requires a funded research project of the scale proposed.

In order to create a list of sub-questions, consider the things you 'need to know' in order to solve the overall problem. Then match each of these things you 'need to know' with specific research activities that provide answers to each of them. This gives you the basic structure of your project.

Creating sub-questions may be a stage in the research design process that you perform automatically. If you work in a field that uses experimental methods, your research project probably falls into a 'need to know' pattern as you develop a set of hypotheses and the activity that tests them.

In contrast, archival, theoretical or desk researchers may not find this process so straightforward. However, the ability to break your project down into a list of things we 'need to know' and activities that 'will tell us' the answers is a very effective way to show that your research is dependent on external funding. The following example shows how this can be done.

## HUMANITIES PROJECT STRUCTURE

This is an extract from a fellowship application by a researcher in the humanities. Although the major project resource is investigator time, the proposed project is structured as carefully as a large-scale experimental project with multiple resources:

> Animation's widespread and diverse impact makes it ideal to study the following questions:
>
> Q. 1: What does it mean to claim that technology participates or has agency in making images?
> Q. 2: Can a technological interface generate an audio-visual language?
> Q. 3: Does the language of an interface inform us about how our view of the world is evolving?
>
> The project will be undertaken in four stages. Stages One and Three develop the theoretical ideas underlying the project: situated action and language of the interface. Stages Two and Four involve working with animations, games and websites to expand and reflect on these theoretical insights. *Digital Media Fellowship*

Using a 'scientific' project structure for a humanities project in this way has advantages. By breaking down the fellowship into three distinct sub-questions and four clearly articulated project components, the applicant immediately gives funding agency decision makers a justification for their investment.

Another category of project that may not fit the standard 'need to know' model is applied research, in which the outcomes are interventions or tools. In this case, you may wish to emphasise what we need to 'develop' rather than 'know'.

## APPLIED PROJECT

The next example, from a complex, multi-partner project, lists the mechanisms needed to ensure effective ways of testing software and achieve the aims of the project. In each case, the applicants' match the solution 'we need' with the tool that the research team 'will provide'.

> Property-driven development is a powerful new mechanism for gaining assurance of system reliability and functionality. However, in order to deliver its full benefits we need tools to integrate property-based testing into the development life cycle.

**Property discovery**. Current testing is based on sets of test cases embedded in test suites; we will provide tools to aid the software developers to extract properties from this test data. Current specifications and models are often informal: we will develop specialised property languages to ease the formalisation of existing specifications.

**Test and property evolution**. All software systems are subject to change and evolution; we will provide tools to support the evolution of tests and properties in line with the evolution of the system itself.

**Property monitoring**. Not all properties can be tested in advance of systems being executed; not all faults will be found during testing, be it ever so thorough. We will also provide tools to support the *post hoc* examination of trace details for conformance to (or indeed violation of) particular constraints.

**Analysing concurrent systems**. At the heart of service oriented systems is *concurrency*: servers will provide services to multiple clients in a seamlessly concurrent way; services will federate to provide complex functionality through concurrently performing parts of a task. We will provide tools by which such concurrent systems can be analysed for fundamental properties. *Software Testing European Project*

If the idea of articulating what we 'need to know' still causes you problems, the following Tool may help. It shows how to break your overall question and research programme into matching lists of sub-questions and research activity components.

---

================================= TOOL 12 ================================

## WHAT DO WE NEED TO KNOW?

This Tool is designed to help break your project into three to five research sub-questions and matching activity components.

1  List your research question and the activity you must undertake to answer it. 'Writing my book' does not count as research activity in this context. You should list all the research activity needed to answer the question. This might include interviews, archive visits, desk research, calculations, experiments, field trips, surveys or practice-as-research activity.

2  When you have made your list, consider how this activity falls into different categories, which might include:

  • Visits to different archives or countries
  • Experiments or interviews with different categories of participant
  • Different experimental conditions
  • Different themes that may emerge from your data
  • Distinct categories or sources of data
  • Different historical periods or sites of investigation
  • Different phases or stages of research activity

3 Group your activity into three to five categories that answer a specific part of the research question. These are your sub-questions.
4 Find a label that identifies each thing that we 'need to know'. Use this phrase consistently across the sub-questions, objectives, headings and within the description of each component of research activity. Always refer to both your 'need to know' sub-questions and their corresponding activity components in the same order.

Use the Tests in Chapter 11 to check whether your project breakdown is logical and likely to succeed in answering the overall research question.

## Section 3: This project is the solution

By this stage, your readers are excited about your research question, convinced that the problem needs solving and that you and your approach may offer the best solution. Your next task is to support the *success*, *competence* and *value* propositions in full by describing your project and its outputs.

In your 'we have a problem' section you outlined your approach and provided evidence for your choice of methodology and project structure. In 'this project is the solution' you explain precisely how you will conduct the research and communicate the knowledge you produce.

'This project is the solution' will form the longest section of the case for support (at least 50 per cent) and funding agency headings may include 'Research Methods', 'Plan of Investigation', 'Research Activity' or 'Study Design'. Sections of the template that deal with outputs and dissemination include headings such as 'Beneficiaries', 'End Users', 'Impact' or 'Exploitation'.

This is the section of the case for support that applicants often neglect. It is essential that you give a full description of your project. The description of research activity and outputs must be complete if you are to convince the referees and grants' committee that your project is the solution.

## Objectives

The 'this project is the solution' section of your case for support must convince decision makers that the proposed project will answer the question. It uses a detailed description of the research programme to do this and referees read it particularly closely.

In order for non-specialist readers to agree that 'your project is the solution', you need to explain in detail:

- Your overall research design and methods
- How you will conduct each individual specific component of research activity (including specific methodological details and an account of resources you needed)
- The timing/duration of each research activity component and an explanation of how the project will be managed
- What you will do with the knowledge you produce

## Stage One: Overall research design and methods

Your first task within this section is to describe your research design in detail. Many funding agencies make a separate section on methodology a specific requirement.

However, you should try to keep the section on general methods as short as possible. It is much easier to understand a description of research methods in the context of a specific piece of research designed to answer a specific question.

Here are two examples of how funded applications introduce their methodology section. Both provide an overview of the general approach and a summary of the project structure.

---

EXAMPLE 17

---

## INTRODUCING METHODS

The following extracts are both taken from the opening lines of the applicants' 'Research Methods' section.

> Our requirements analysis and early development will be based on two existing Semantic Web projects, both tackling complex real-world problems at the leading edge of eScience (workflows in bioinformatics, medical orders). Later in the project, a third application will be developed from scratch in a different domain (travel), suitable for incorporation into the University of Manchester's advanced OWL tutorial. *Web Authoring Project*

> The project will be undertaken in four stages. Stages One and Three develop the theoretical ideas that underlie the project: situated action and language of the interface. Stages Two and Four involve working with animations, games and websites to expand and reflect on these theoretical insights. My research method is to combine analysis of moving images with an investigation of contextual materials such as published interviews and software manuals and interviews with image-makers. *Digital Media Fellowship*

In each case, the project structure is based on the sub-questions, ensuring that the reader receives consistent messages about the planned activity.

---

Even if the same methods are used in more than one of the sections of the research project it may be easier for the reader to understand them if they are described in the context of the first specific piece of research in which they will be used. Subsequent components that use the same method can then refer readers back to the earlier description.

However, if your project uses a complex experimental design, it may also be worthwhile to summarise common features in the introductory section so that you do not need to repeat 'technical' information several times.

---

EXAMPLE 18

## SAVING SPACE

This example uses the introduction to the 'Methods' section to demonstrate common methodological features of seven proposed experiments:

> All seven experiments follow the same structure (cf. Figure 2): they examine the long-term retention of newly consolidated knowledge, as a function of whether or not that knowledge is reactivated just before learning similar information. As shown section 2.2.1, this approach has been successful in revealing reconsolidation effects in various forms of memory in both animals and humans.
>
> The features common to all experiments are as described below:
>
> 1   On day 1, participants are explicitly instructed to learn two sets (A and B) of fictitious words (sometimes with their meaning) through intense exposure ....
> 2   Twenty-four hours later, and thus after overnight consolidation, participants first rehearse half of the words they learnt the day before (set A, for instance).
> 3   Immediately afterwards they learn two new sets of fictitious words, similar in form or meaning to the sets A and B words. Consequently, participants have now for each A or B word a potential 'corruptor' word, i.e., $A_{cor}$ or $B_{cor}$, in memory... etc. *Memory Research Project*

---

### Stage Two: Specific activity components

By the time referees and grants' committee members reach this stage of your case for support, they will be clear about your project structure and ready to understand how you will conduct each component of research activity.

After introducing your general method, you should describe each of the research activity components. By now, these headings should be immediately recognisable to readers as they use the same labels and are presented in the same order as the research sub-questions.

---

This is the most important part of your entire research grant application as it is only here that you describe in full what you intend to do and how you will use the grant provided by the funding agency. If your explanation is inadequate or unclear, the decision makers will not be able to support your project, however convinced they are of its importance and your capabilities.

As a rule of thumb, you should aim to include enough detail for the project to be replicated. No matter how eminent you are, you need to provide this basic information. Nothing is taken on trust by critical referees.

The information your case for support provides about each activity component should include:

- The research sub-question or thing you 'need to know'
- When the activity takes place and its duration
- Who conducts the activity, where it takes place and which project resources it involves
- A detailed description of the research activity that answers each sub-question or thing we 'need to know'
- What the activity 'will tell us' and how you will arrive at your answer with the information you gather

Although there may be a separate justification of costs section, you make your job easier if you do not consign this information to an appendix. Referees and grants' committee members are more likely to support your request if you show how each resource is used alongside the activity it relates to. Also mention resources provided by the institution to show that the research environment is appropriate.

## Stage Three: What you will do with the knowledge

The final part of the 'this project is the solution' element of your case for support explains how the information derived from the research will be made available to its beneficiaries.

Research on a topic that has direct economic, health or social benefit should contain a component that will allow that benefit to be realised. It is important that you are specific and realistic about the likely outputs. If any outputs have inherent costs (e.g. designing a website, hosting a conference) these should be included in the budget. All dissemination activity that takes place within the life of the project should also be included in the timetable.

If you conduct pure 'blue skies' research then this part is mostly about academic dissemination through conferences and papers. Even if your project has immediate benefit only for academic audiences, your referees and grants' committee members will want to understand its eventual potential for social and economic benefit.

EXAMPLE 19

## PROJECT OUTCOMES

These extracts illustrate two approaches to communicating project outcomes within the narrative of a case for support. The first describes the knowledge that will be generated and the implications of this. The second example emphasises the disciplines that will be interested in the findings and lists the ways in which outcomes will be communicated to academics in these fields.

> The product of the proposed research will be a much better understanding of the architecture of the system that accomplishes language comprehension. These studies will provide a much more detailed picture of how the mental lexicon changes over both the short term, and the longer term. Such an understanding is critical to our understanding of language processing. In turn, because language is such a fundamental cognitive ability, progress in describing language processing will enhance our understanding of human cognition, under both normal and disordered conditions. *Spoken Word Project*

> The research carried out in this project will be of interest to cinema studies, communication and media studies, science and technology studies and also practice-based research. It will be written up as 4 journal articles (potential publishers include *Body and Society, Convergence, Journal of Visual Culture, Journal of Media Practice*). My research findings will be presented at three conferences: Society for Animation Studies, Society of the Social Studies of Science, and the Society for Cinema and Media Studies. *Digital Media Fellowship*

This difference in emphasis is appropriate to the nature of the two projects. The first applicant requests money from a government agency that funds research into human health and is more interested in the practical benefits than high-impact publications. The second project is theoretical and communication of the findings within a wide research community is the priority.

---

# Conclusion

This chapter suggests ways of streamlining the application process and communicating with decision makers more effectively by understanding the underlying functions of the application template and generic properties of an effective case for support. By following the advice in this chapter, you should now have a generic structure for your case for support that can be mapped on to individual agency templates.

# EIGHT

## HOW TO EXPLOIT THE APPLICATION TEMPLATE

## Summary

This chapter shows you how to adapt the generic structure described in Chapter 7 to the relevant funding agency template. It also provides a system for identifying the relationship between the case for support and wider template that shows where you can replicate, summarise or expand your arguments and evidence.

These two functions make the process of presenting your project within a set application template more straightforward and efficient. A series of extracts from successful grant applications illustrate some of the advice and guidance in this chapter. You can find more information about each of these in Appendix 3.

## Introduction

The previous chapter explains how every case for support has a set of generic functions that help get your 'foot in the door', convince readers that 'we have a problem' and demonstrate that 'your project is the solution'. This structure can be summarised as follows:

## A foot in the door

- The research question
- Importance of question
- Project preview

## We have a problem

- This problem needs solving
- You have the skills and experience to solve this problem
- The proposed project is the best way to solve this problem

## This project is the solution

- Overall research design and methods
- Project components: methods, activity, timing, resources
- Timing and project management
- What you will do with the knowledge

Your next task is to adapt this structure to the funding agency application template. In order to do this, you need to know what sort of information to include and where to put it.

We already know that agency templates vary widely. As an applicant armed with a generic project structure and presented with the agency template, you face one or more of the following challenges:

- Fitting the generic structure to a specific application template
- Creating the optimum layout for your case for support where the agency's guidance is non-specific
- Deciding how information should be distributed across the case for support, the application form and any appendices
- Dealing with additional information not (apparently) included in the generic structure
- Dealing with mandatory sections of the template that seem inappropriate or irrelevant to your project

Each of these will be dealt with in turn in this chapter.

# Highly-specific application templates

Many funding agencies have specific and idiosyncratic templates. The next example shows the variations in one 'family' of related agencies, the UK's Research Councils.

EXAMPLE 20

## DIFFERENT TEMPLATES

The following table shows the extent of variation among a selection of funding agencies, in this case UK Research Councils. This simplified table does not reflect application form variations, individual funding scheme requirements or any of the optional attachments specified by each funding agency.

| UK RESEARCH COUNCILS[26] | | | |
|---|---|---|---|
| Funder | MRC | ESRC | AHRC |
| Limit | 3–12 pages | 6–12 pages | 2,000–3,000 words |
| Case for Support | Title | Title | Title |
| | 1  Importance | 1  Introduction | 1  Research Questions |
| | 2  Scientific Potential | 2  Research Questions | 2  Research Context |
| | 2.1 People and Track Record | 3  Proposed Research Methods | 3  Research Methods |
| | 2.2 Environment | 4  Data Collection: Datasets Review | 4  Project Management |
| | 2.3 Research Plans | 5  Data Collection: Details | 5  Dissemination |
| | 3  Ethics and Research Governance | 6  Data Collection: Potential Problems | |
| | 4  Data Preservation and Sharing | 7  Data Analysis | |
| | 5  Public Engagement in Science | 8  Risk Mitigation | |
| | 6  Exploitation and Dissemination | 9  Choice of Discipline | |
| Required Attachments | Pathways to Impact | Pathways to Impact | Pathways to Impact |
| | Justification of Resources | Justification of Resources | Justification of Resources |
| | CV | CV | CV |
| | | | Publication List |

---

[26]https://jes.rcuk.ac.uk/Handbook/Index.htm#pages/GuidanceonCompletingaStandardG/ CaseforSupportandAttachments/ESRCSpecificRequirements.htm (last accessed 10 April 2012)

| Funder | BBSRC | EPSRC | NERC |
|---|---|---|---|
| Page Limit | 6 plus | 8 | 8 |
| Case for Support | Title | Title | Title |
| | 1A Track record and contribution to UK competitiveness | 1 Track record (two sides) | |
| | 1B Statement on data sharing | | |
| | 1C Statement on use of animals | | |
| | 2 Background | 2 Background | 1 Track Record |
| | 2.1 Topic and Context | 3 Academic Impact | 2 Programme of Research |
| | 2.2 Past and Current Work on Topic | 4 Research Hypotheses and Objectives | 2.1 Rationale |
| | 3 Programme | 5 Programme and Methodology | 2.2 Objectives |
| | 3.1 Aims and Objectives | 6 References | 2.3 Methodology and Approach |
| | 3.2 Methodology | | 2.4 Programme and Plan of Research |
| | 3.3 Timeliness and Novelty | | 2.5 Project Management |
| | 3.4 Programme of Work | | 2.6 Datasets |
| | 4 References | | |
| Required Attachments | Pathways to Impact | Pathways to Impact | Pathways to Impact |
| | Justification of Resources | Justification of Resources | Justification of Resources |
| | CV | Previous Track Record Workplan | CV |

The variations are further exaggerated by the idiosyncratic use of headings. For example, the headings used in the EPRSC case for support template are completely different from the AHRC's headings even though the two documents have the same basic function. Equally, if you read the guidance for the AHRC section on 'Research Methods', you will see that this section incorporates details of the programme of research that other Research Councils request under different headings.

For more detail on how to find this sort of information about your target funding agencies, please refer to Appendix 2.

This means that you must always read the funding agency guidance carefully and with the aim of understanding the function as well as the title of each template section.

The advantage of the generic approach is that it is easier to decipher a template when you know about the three underlying functions, which each support one or more of the four key propositions. This understanding will help you read the template and guidance and identify where different parts of your argument and evidence should go.

## Non-specific application templates

If the funding agency gives you complete freedom to structure the case for support, you need to make your own decisions and are free to follow the generic structure closely. Before you do this, read the agency guidance closely and list its evaluation criteria.

A funding agency that invites proposals for applied projects in matters of social welfare (e.g. the Nuffield Foundation[27]) will require slightly different headings and emphases from one that prioritises an innovative approach and scholarly outcomes (e.g. Leverhulme Trust[28]).

We suggest the following as a rough guide:

- Call the 'foot in the door' section 'Introduction'. Keep it short. It should be less than 20 per cent of the case for support.
- Call the 'we have a problem' section 'Background to the Project'. Keep it to less than 30 per cent of the case for support.
- Call the 'this project is the solution' section 'Programme of Research'. Make sure that it is at least 50 per cent of the case for support.
- Ensure that you also include sections on dissemination, your project timetable and a justification of resources.

## Distributing information across templates

Whether the funding agency template is highly specific or unstructured, it is likely that you can recycle some information from your case for support and use it in other sections of the application template.

This normally takes three forms:

- Whole sections of text that you can re-use word for word
- Text that you must expand to provide the additional detail required by particular appendices
- Elements that you must summarise elsewhere

[27]www.nuffieldfoundation.org (last accessed 20 October 2011)
[28]www.leverhulme.ac.uk (last accessed 20 October 2011)

It is important that you never treat these sections of the wider template as an excuse to save word count in your case for support and completely leave out part of your argument. No decision maker should have to hunt through appendices or your application form in order to find evidence that shows how you meet any of the agency's evaluation criteria.

Consequently, all information that contributes to a positive evaluation, according to funding agency criteria, must appear in the case for support. You may opt for an abbreviated discussion (with reference to the relevant section of the wider template), but if you banish important information to an appendix it may go unnoticed.

The application form and appendices give you the chance to restate, refine or amplify key information and arguments. In preparing these parts of the application template it is important to present information in a way that reinforces the case for support. Failure to do so risks confusing and weakening your arguments.

There are two guidelines for reinforcement:

- Re-use text whenever possible. This is good for readers, because they are more likely to remember something if exactly the same words are used to describe it more than once. It is also good for the writer because you have to generate less text.
- Whenever you repeat a list of items, keep the order exactly the same.

Refer to Appendix 2 for a useful guide to the relationship between elements of the case for support and the wider application template.

# Additional information

Most funding agency templates contain sections that require information not included in the 'generic' case for support structure. These cannot be dealt with by replicating, expanding or summarising information.

These sections usually reflect either:

- Discipline-specific requirements (e.g. ethics, research environment) that affect the potential success of the project and, therefore, support the *success* proposition
- The requirements of funding agency stakeholders (e.g. public engagement with science, impact) that contribute to the *importance* and *value* propositions

The nature of a particular agency's appendices also gives you some insight into its priorities. You must treat them seriously and accept that the funding agency will use this information to decide whether your project justifies the relevant propositions.

If the additional information is essential to any evaluation criteria, you should also refer to it in the main case for support. The following example from a successful application shows how a discussion of research ethics is incorporated into the case for support narrative:

---

## INCORPORATING ETHICS

In this example, a discussion of research ethics in the methodology section of the case for support is used to strengthen the applicants' decision to use secondary data sources.

> The main challenges stem from the secretive nature of rendition and the sensitivity of the material. The research will be based on documentary sources rather than engagement with human subjects. This is a deliberate move intended to limit any further suffering that interviewing victims of rendition might produce, since the interview process can be highly traumatic for victims of torture, as it forces them to relive their experiences, and can even emulate the interrogation process.
>
> Since detainees that have been released have given lengthy testimonies to their lawyers, there is no need to further subject them to trauma by re-interviewing them, especially, as has already been the case, individuals have been willing for their testimonies to be released by their lawyers. Nevertheless, it may be that some of the testimonies need to be treated as confidential materials, with only certain levels of attribution permitted. In such cases, careful attention will be paid to the instructions of the lawyers in question and their clients regarding the use of material, including ensuring the anonymity of informants as requested, carefully protecting their data, and ensuring the safe storage of any such testimonies. *Rendition and Detention Project*

This discussion of ethics in the case for support supports the 'success' proposition in demonstrating this approach is likely to answer the question in the most appropriate and effective way.

### 'Irrelevant' requirements

You may also come across sections of the application template that seem inappropriate, completely irrelevant or that seem to distort your account of the project. If this is the case, one of the following usually applies:

- The section is genuinely irrelevant and you will not be penalised for stating this (e.g. ethical review for a project with no human participants or animals)

---

THE RESEARCH FUNDING TOOLKIT

- You need to adapt your design or rethink elements of the project in order to meet mandatory requirements (e.g. impact, public engagement, project management)
- Your project is unsuitable for this funding agency and you should reconsider your application

If you cannot decide which of the above applies to you, turn to the detailed funding agency guidance or evaluation criteria for more information. Alternatively, contact the agency secretariat or – best of all – an experienced grants' committee member. They will advise on the status of the section in question.

There are three particular elements in the average application template that researchers often find problematic: the timetable, the project management section and the impact statement.

## Workplans and timetables

Applicants often feel that it is impossible to predict when each element of activity will take place and how long each component will take. There is no way round this. The funding agency expects you to be confident and specific about what you will do, who will do it, when you will do it and how long it will take.

Your best bet is to give the most plausible account you can of your research programme. If there are good reasons why you cannot adhere to you original plan and the changes do not contravene funding agency regulations, you may well have some flexibility during the life of the project.

However, the timetable in your application document will be closely scrutinised and an unrealistic approximation will lose you the grant. Ensure that you calculate and justify your potential timings carefully.

EXAMPLE 22

## FELLOWSHIP TIMETABLE

The following timetable for an extended research visit by an overseas scholar helps justify the length of the fellowship and the overall value of the visit:

Part 1 (a shorter phase) is preparatory. It will lay the foundation for the more extended practical project to follow in May/June. Preparation will involve:

- initial casting
- collation of research materials and texts for devising
- 3 research seminars
- 2 Leverhulme lectures
- the setting of tasks to be pursued by students under staff supervision.

Part 2 is focused on realising the practice-as-research project. It will involve the following stages:

- 6 weeks of devising rehearsals punctuated by weekly Leverhulme lecture/presentations that draw from and comment on the creative process
- consultation sessions with individual practitioner/researchers to tease out responses to the work and their reflections on moments of practice
- presentation of a public performance at the School of Arts summer festival over 3 nights
- post-performance reflection and wider dissemination linked to the presentation of documentation. *Theatre and Performance Visiting Fellowship*

In many cases, the timetable for a project is only created because the funding agency requires one in the application template. You may find that this expectation enhances your project design as it forces you to consider the likely timing and order of each activity component.

## Project management

Funding agency decision makers do not assume that your project will run smoothly without evidence to support your claims. If your project is of sufficient scale and the funding agency requires it, you will be expected to articulate your plans for formal project management. If your proposed research is complex, proper project management will be an important way of justifying your *success* proposition.

This is not a task to take on the day before your deadline. Depending on the project, you may realise that you need to recruit a steering group, budget for regular project meetings and come up with a convincing project management schedule.

This can take a considerable time and should be incorporated into your project design stage rather than left until the last minute. Properly planned, high-profile project management activity also enhances the impact of your research and helps convince readers that your project is important (i.e. the *importance* and *value* propositions).

 EXAMPLE 23

## THE IMPORTANT ADVISORY BOARD

The *Web Authoring Project* case for support presents the impressive advisory board below the project title and is very effective in establishing the importance of the project and impressing decision makers as they start reading:

SEMANTIC WEB AUTHORING TOOL (SWAT)

Investigators: Richard Power, Donia Scott (Open University); Robert Stevens, Alan Rector (Manchester)

Advisory Board: Bedirhan Ustun (World Health Organization); Sam Brandt (Siemens); Catherine Dolbear (Ordnance Survey); Ken Lunn (NHS, Connecting for Health); Mark Musen (Stanford); Carole Goble (Manchester). *Web Authoring Project*

In this case, including such an impressive Advisory Board as a sub-title of the application helps the 'foot in the door' task by capturing the attention of readers and exciting them about the potential reach of the project.

A formal project management programme can also help convince decision makers in other ways, as the next example shows:

EXAMPLE 24

## INTEGRATING PROJECT MANAGEMENT

The multi-partner *Software Testing European Project* assigns project management its own work package and set of objectives.

The objectives of the management structure and policies are:

1  to ensure timely delivery of expected results
2  to implement the communication procedures for reporting and reviewing
3  to undertake contingency planning – identifying and analysing any potential risks, and to determine an appropriate action plan to minimise such risks
4  to organise project workshops and interact with relevant open source and standardisation initiatives
5  to coordinate with related EU and national projects including relevant STREP, IPs and NoEs
6  to monitor any gender, ethical and other socio-economic issues arising in the project. *Software Testing European Project*

This application makes explicit uses of the project management work programme to support both the *success* and *value* propositions. In both of these examples, project management arrangements are integral to the project design.

## Impact and engagement

Impact and Public Engagement requirements ask you to show how your project may benefit non-academic beneficiaries. In most cases, you will be expected to specify a formal programme of activity that communicates your outcomes beyond academic circles.

This is problematic for many researchers but exceptions from impact requirements may only be made for limited categories of 'blue skies' projects. In any case, you may find it hard to excite non-specialist readers if you can make no link between your research and the possibility of social, health or economic benefit.

A complete lack of economic and social impact at any level may cause difficulties in your efforts to support the *importance* proposition.

Consequently, you may have no choice in this matter. The funding agency provides guidance on the sort of information and activity that is acceptable. You should read this at an early stage in the application development process and build in relevant, specific initiatives to your overall project design.

A last-minute description of cosmetic, implausible impact activity directed at vague or unrealistic audiences (such as 'a newsletter for senior politicians') is likely to damage your chances.

---

EXAMPLE 25

## REALISTIC IMPACT

The *Memory Research Project* provides a good example of how the applicant takes a piece of basic research and provides realistic and specific arrangements to communicate the results outside academia.

> Work Programme One will lead to several publications in high-impact psychology journals, such as *Psychological Science, Cognition, Journal of Experimental Psychology: Learning, Memory and Cognition*, or *Learning and Memory*. Findings will also be presented at conferences such as the Conference of the European Society for Cognitive Psychology (Europe, Aug 2013), the Annual Meeting of the Psychonomic Society (USA, Nov 2012, 2013 and 2014), and the Congress of International Association of Applied Linguistics (Worldwide, 2014). Work Programmes Two will be disseminated in high-impact journals such as *Journal of Neuroscience, Journal of Cognitive Neuroscience*, or *Neurobiology of Learning and Memory*, and conferences such as the Cognitive Neuroscience Society Annual Meeting (USA, 2014) and the Neurobiology of Language Conference (USA, 2014).
>
> On the applied front, initial discussions have taken place with commercial language tuition providers, Rosetta Stone™, to show them how my research findings could contribute to the tuition softwares they devise. Yearly meetings with their research team led by Dr. Duane Sider are planned for the whole duration of the project.
>
> To reach non-academic research users, the BCBL website will also regularly post news from the project, and media activities with relevant trade journals (such as *Teachers Magazine* in the UK; *Periodismo Científico y Divulgativo* and

*Psicología y Educación* in Spain), science new agencies (such as *Basqueresearch* and *Alphagalileo*) are planned. Furthermore, towards the end of the project, a one-day workshop on the issue of language learning and reconsolidation will be hosted by the BCBL. It will feature five invited speakers, including two speakers from the BCBL, two speakers from the UK and one speaker from the US. It is impossible at this stage to be precise as to format and number of attendees, but we plan 30 self-funded participants. *Memory Research Project*

Note that industry contacts are mentioned by name, as are the titles of non-academic publications that might find the work of interest.

---

EXAMPLE 26

## REALISTIC PUBLIC ENGAGEMENT

The potentially controversial *Research Animal Project* shows an appropriate level of public engagement activity for a project that could be dangerous to the Principal Investigator if communicated to a wider public.

**Public Engagement in Science**: Members of the research group regularly give presentations on developing improved strategies for optimising animal welfare, and have participated in poster presentations to MPs and MEPs, and maintain a website (www.ahwla.org.uk) to disseminate our own and others' results in animal welfare research. *Research Animal Project*

Once more, specific details and link to a website are provided to reassure referees and committee members that the engagement activity has been actively considered and that the proposed activity is appropriate, realistic and achievable.

---

# Conclusion

After reading this chapter, you should have a set of techniques that help you take your 'generic' case for support and map it quickly and effectively on to a specific funding agency template. You will also know how to extract elements of the case for support and repeat, summarise or expand them elsewhere in your application template. The next chapter deals with developing the right arguments and evidence to support your key propositions and to show that your project meets all the evaluation criteria.

# NINE

## HOW TO CONVINCE DECISION MAKERS: ARGUMENTS AND EVIDENCE

## Summary

This chapter helps you convince referees and grants' committee members to support your research grant application by creating the right arguments and supporting evidence. It also explains how to present your arguments in ways that are easy to understand and remember.

There are two Tools at the end of this chapter. *Produce Your Evidence* helps you generate the arguments and evidence that form the building blocks of your application document. *Arguments and Evidence: the 10 Step Process* provides a step-by-step approach to building and structuring your argument.

In addition, you will find further extracts from the series of successful grant applications throughout this chapter. You can find more information about each of these in Appendix 3.

## Introduction

A research grant application describes a research project and convinces the reader that the proposed activity is worth the sum requested. The funding agency awards you a grant if the grants' committee is convinced that your project is better than others in the same competition.

Referees and grants' committee members usually evaluate projects using the application document alone. Consequently, the arguments and evidence you choose to include are crucial to the outcome.

In order to help present your case well, the funding agency usually specifies an application template together with detailed guidance on what to include. Describing your project within the strict constraints of a set template presents three technical challenges:

1  Including the right information within the appropriate sections of the application document.
2  Describing the proposed project within a rigid (and sometimes inconvenient) template.
3  Restricting information about your project to the prescribed page limits and word counts.

Meeting these challenges simultaneously is demanding and can detract from the main aim of grant-writing, which is to produce a convincing application. Unfortunately, applicants often struggle so hard to meet the three 'technical' criteria that they fail to create a strong overall argument.

Creating a strong argument is important because grants' committee members and referees will not share your enthusiasm for the research question or understand the nuances of your field. They have limited time to spend reading your application document but are expected to evaluate it using a rigid set of criteria.

If you participate in some of the group-based tests in Chapter 11, you will understand what it is like to act as a referee or grants' committee member.

Unfortunately, many applicants never appreciate the challenges faced by funding agency decision makers and make poor choices about the information they include in their research grant applications. Common mistakes include:

• Including a lengthy discussion of the overall research topic and literature that offers wide-ranging insights into the field but does not explain why the question is important, why the project is likely to succeed or why the applicants are competent
• Failing to include a sufficiently detailed account of the proposed research programme
• Presenting arguments that are relevant to the applicants' discipline rather than to funding agency criteria.

These mistakes risk irritating readers by including irrelevant information or frustrating them by leaving out important information.

## Four key propositions

The generic application structure proposed in Chapter 7 is based on four key propositions that every fundable research grant application must make. If you keep the four propositions in mind as you develop and choose application content, you will help keep your arguments on track.

The four key propositions are:

1  The *importance* proposition: this proposal asks an important question.
2  The *success* proposition: this project is likely to answer the question.
3  The *value* proposition: the likely gain from this project is worth the resources requested.
4  The *competence* proposition: the applicant and team are competent to carry out the project as described.

Everything you include in the final draft of your application must support one of your key propositions and you must support each proposition with a range of objective evidence.

In addition, there may be secondary propositions that relate to individual funding agency criteria or the nature of your research. For example, secondary to the competence proposition, you may also need to convince decision makers that your institution will provide an appropriate research environment. Alternatively, as part of the success proposition, the way you disseminate results to non-academic audiences may be crucial.

The clarity of the evidence you provide is also crucial because the decision makers are not specialists in your area and generally have little prior knowledge or natural enthusiasm for your work. The task of critical referees and busy grants' committee members is to find evidence for and against the key propositions.

In summary, here are three things you must do in order to justify your four propositions effectively:

1  Produce the right information and evidence.
2  Help busy readers find the information they need.
3  Help readers understand and remember the information you present.

The rest of this chapter helps you do this.

## The right information and evidence

The application template limits the amount of information you can include about your project, especially as font size and margin width are usually prescribed by the funding agency. Consequently, you will always have to make choices about what information to include or exclude.

The *Produce Your Evidence* Tool at the end of this chapter shows you how to generate arguments and evidence to support your four key propositions and any additional agency-specific requirements. Meanwhile, the *Arguments and Evidence* Tool provides a step-by-step approach that takes you from reading the evaluation criteria through to testing your application document before submission.

Producing the right information and evidence can be particularly problematic in relation to the 'this project is the solution' section of your case for support. You know that the referees and grants' committee members are not especially expert in your field. However, the precise nature of their ignorance can only be loosely predicted. This is one of the reasons that luck plays a part in whether your application wins funding.

In these circumstances, your best option is to:

- Describe the proposed research activity in such detail that a colleague could replicate the project using your application document alone (see Test 6 in Chapter 11)
- Identify the aspects of your proposed project most likely to attract criticism from related fields and provide evidence that defends against them (see Test 9 in Chapter 11)

As 'this project is the solution' is where you explain in detail what you will do with the grant, this is the most important section of your application for the serious detail-readers. Aim to devote at least half of your case for support to this section.

## Finding important information

In the context of research grant applications, it is dangerous to assume that busy referees and grants' committee members will read every word of your application.

In truth, busy speed-readers may skip certain sections of your application document completely. If you want them to remember your main argument and supporting evidence you will need to position key messages carefully and repeat them. Appendix 2 provides an overview and analysis of the function and content of typical application templates. The next chapter also offers advice on how to position key messages as prominently as possible.

If you produce a high-quality application, you can expect that:

- Referees will read every sentence and pay special attention to the programme of research.
- Designated grants' committee members will read in full the referee reports, the summary and the budget. They will also speed-read the case for support.
- The wider grants' committee membership will read your summary, glance at the budget and flick through the rest of the document.

This means that certain parts of your application document are more likely to be read than others. The project summary and budget total sit firmly at the top of the hierarchy.

In addition, speed-readers are more likely to read the first sentence of a section or paragraph than the last. Consequently, important messages must always come first. This gives readers their best chance of reading and remembering your key arguments and evidence.

---

EXAMPLE 27

## 'SPEED-READABLE' PARAGRAPHS

The *Theatre and Performance Visiting Fellowship* proposal caters for the speed-reader in a paragraph that justifies the choice of fellow. The first sentence provides the key message:

> Schechner is a leading scholar in theatre and performance studies, which he, along with others, founded, and for which he is recognised globally. He has published widely with his books translated into 14 languages. Schechner is editor-in-chief of *The Drama Review*, the world's leading performance studies journal. He is the recipient of numerous awards, including Lifetime Achievement from Performance Studies international, Lifetime Career Achievement from the American Theatre in Higher Education association; he holds two honorary doctorates (Hong Kong and Romania). The "Richard Schechner Center" at the Shanghai Theatre Academy is named in his honour. He has taught, lectured, and directed in every continent except Antarctica. His academic renown is coupled with a long track record in theatre-making as a director/devisor. He has appeared in the UK at conferences speaking on specialist subjects but this will be the first time he has presented his 'broad spectrum' approach in a systematic and sustained way in the UK. It will also be the first time Schechner has created a piece of work here. His presence will attract a huge amount of interest, not just at Kent but across the UK and Europe, where he has recently been an Erasmus Mundus Fellow. *Theatre and Performance Visiting Fellowship*

---

You make your paragraphs work better if you remember the difference between the 'convincing' and the 'defensive' elements of your arguments. In summary:

- Good convincing arguments help referees and grants' committee members support your application. This category of argument must be actively remembered.
- Defensive arguments help referees (in particular) forget their criticisms. This category of argument can be forgotten once it has done its job.
- Defensive arguments are directed at referees who read everything and can be less prominently positioned. There is one exception. If your project is high risk or has unusual features, then defensive arguments may also apply to grants' committee members and should be given more prominence.

The following examples look at two cases in which applicants need to use defensive arguments very prominently.

---

EXAMPLE 28

## THE PROMINENT DEFENCE

This five-year multi-experiment application takes the unusual approach of taking a defensive approach in the opening lines of the 'Research Design and Methods' section. The applicant addresses the absence of certain methodological details and the necessity for flexibility in the overall design over the life of the project:

> In the following sections, we will describe the experiments we propose to conduct in continuing our research on spoken language. We ask that readers extend a certain amount of trust in two respects: (1) The descriptions of the experiments do not include details such as the number of trials or number of subjects; we believe that we can be trusted to implement designs with appropriate choices for such parameters. (2) The described experiments represent our best current plans. As the work proceeds over the next several years, we expect to modify the designs and add new experiments, as new results improve our understanding. Our prior work suggests that the product that emerges will be enhanced by such a process of development. *Spoken Word Project*

In the next example, the applicant defends using animals in medical research. As this is such an emotive and controversial issue, the applicant does so in the most prominent position in the application, which is the project summary.

> The use of animals in medical research is a highly sensitive topic and in many cases the public perception is that this should not be allowed. Replacement strategies have been suggested such as culturing tumours outside of the body and then testing anticancer treatments. However, as scientists we know it is currently more appropriate to use animals as drugs that might combat cancer in people could behave very differently when tested in culture. Where animals are used we have a moral and legal obligation to minimise pain and suffering. *Research Animal Project*

In summary, if defensive information is an essential part of your argument, you need to position it where it is most likely to be seen by busy speed-readers.

---

## Understandable, memorable information

Whatever the quality and accessibility of the evidence, you will not convince referees and grants' committee members to support your project if your application document is a slow, difficult read. Fundable research grant applications must be memorable and easy to read if they are to stand out against the competition.

In order to make your key arguments and evidence memorable, you must appreciate that the amount of information your readers will retain is limited.

It is better to provide grants' committee members with a few headline messages than a series of convoluted arguments.

One of the most famous papers in Psychology[29] (Miller 1956) points out that we can remember a list of around seven pieces of information without needing to make notes. This means that if you want a referee or committee member to remember the content of a research grant application, you should have no more than seven key messages.

As discussed, there are four key propositions common to any fundable research grant application. However, reducing your entire research programme to this many pieces of information is not a viable option.

Luckily, Miller's famous paper offers a way of extending the limit on the number of items that can be held in the working memory. 'Chunking' is the process of grouping a set of related items together under individual headings. Each heading can be remembered as a single item and the contents 'unpacked' afterwards.

For example, if you have generated four pieces of evidence that show why your methodological approach is likely to be effective, group them together. Bullet points or a numbered list will help present them as a memorable 'chunk' with a shared introductory sentence. This approach is easier to remember than four discursive paragraphs that present each piece of related evidence in isolation.

Evaluating research grant applications is actually rather stressful, especially for the designated committee member. Consequently, we can expect the capacity of the working memory to be reduced in this situation. So the list should have fewer than seven items.

The following examples show how two successful applicants achieved this in practice.

 **EXAMPLE 29**

## CHUNKING

The *Web Authoring Project* uses 'chunking' techniques to break down the overall project into five specific objectives, which are presented as a series of bullet points:

> Our scientific aim is to find principles by which natural and formal languages can be bridged, so obtaining the accessibility of natural language without losing the precision of ontologies and other metadata. Part of this task is to identify

---

[29]Miller, George A. (1956) 'The magical number seven, plus or minus two: some limits on our capacity for processing information'. *Psychological Review* 63 (2): 81–97.

limitations on such a mapping – for instance, it may be that ontologies as well as natural languages must accept certain constraints. From an engineering perspective, we seek practical methods through which a subject-matter expert can view and edit ontologies and other metadata on the Semantic Web, tested in applications of realistic complexity.

To meet these aims, we have the following objectives:

- To understand current authoring practice for ontologies and other metadata represented in OWL/RDF. This will provide requirements for a Semantic Web authoring tool.
- To find principles based on these authoring requirements for bridging between natural language and formal ontologies (and other metadata).
- To provide a format for encoding linguistic resources that supports the mapping of linguistic patterns to ontologies.
- To produce a tool allowing users to extend the mapping of language to ontology without need of expertise in linguistics.
- To produce (by combining the above) a tool for authoring ontologies and other metadata by dire ct manipulation of generated texts, for real-world applications in e-Science, biomedicine, and travel. *Web Authoring Project*

The Digital Media Fellowship takes 'chunking' a step further. The three sub-questions are each broken down into a further two or three parts. If these ten questions were presented without any 'chunking', they would be very difficult to read and understand.

Q. 1: What does it mean to claim that technology participates or has agency in the creation of moving images?

- In what ways does technology transform the actions of human users of technological interfaces?
- How can science and technology studies add to our understanding of hybrid agency in the creation of moving images?
- How can we avoid being overly deterministic with regard to technology?

Q. 2: Can a technological interface generate an audio-visual language?

- Can images have a language derived from the limits and possibilities of a software package?
- Does this language influence what an image-maker can or cannot achieve?

Q. 3: Does the language of an interface inform us about how our view of the world is evolving?

- Does the language of an interface give us insight into how we manage information about the world?
- If an interface privileges an impression of smoothness and ease of movement, does that deny the complexity of the world? *Digital Media Fellowship*

# Conclusion

This chapter emphasises the importance of providing the arguments and evidence that non-specialist decision makers need in order to support your application. It also explains how to present this information in the way that will best help referees and grants' committee members to read, understand and remember it.

The following two Tools help you generate appropriate evidence and provide a step-by-step approach to producing the arguments and evidence you need to meet the evaluation criteria.

---

**TOOL 13**

---

## PRODUCE YOUR EVIDENCE

This Tool suggests categories of evidence to support each of the key propositions. It gives you short sections of text that will form the building blocks of your case for support. Consequently, this Tool is a good way to focus your application on the needs of its readers and ensure that you create a convincing overall argument.

### The *importance* proposition: this proposal asks an important question

In relation to your overall research question:

- Name the academic and/or user communities that will find your answers useful, and demonstrate this with reference to academic literature or policy documents. For example, show that one of the things 'we need to know' is a crucial missing link in an important theoretical argument, or that it meets a social, health or economic need.
- Prove that the questions have not been asked before (provide citations from relevant fields) OR
- Demonstrate that recent important work leads naturally to the question you want to answer (e.g. pilot data, evidence from other fields or from related questions).
- Demonstrate the potential benefits to end users, however theoretical your project.

### The *success* proposition: this project is likely to answer the question

By following the advice in the previous chapter, you should now have three to five sub-questions or things we 'need to know' and a set of matching activity components that 'will tell us' the answer. In relation to each set of sub-question and matching project component:

- Cite research that shows how your chosen methods are appropriate, e.g.
  - They have been used to answer similar questions successfully.
  - Your method is more effective than possible alternatives.
  - If your chosen methods are new, unusual or high risk, provide an argument in favour of your choice with citations.
- Describe each component of the investigation so completely and clearly that a colleague could replicate the project from the application document alone (e.g. describe each experiment, give number and duration of interviews and explain what they will discover, describe the selection of participants, explain the purpose and duration of archive visits). This will help referees and committee members understand how your project is capable of answering the questions.
- Explain what resources (including staff) will be used to carry out each activity.
- Explain exactly how you will analyse data or deal with the information you gather in order to answer your questions successfully.
- Provide a timetable of the project that shows how each phase, component and piece of activity fits together.

## The *value* proposition: the likely gain from this project is worth the resources requested

- Mention each requested resource within your description of the relevant part of your Plan of Investigation.
- Explain why each item is priced at the level requested (e.g. standard institutional rates, as a result of a competitive tender, estimate based on which criteria).
- Explain why you need specific quantities of resource (e.g. proportion of investigator time, number of paid participants, duration and frequency of project travel, number of PhD students).

## The *competence* proposition: the applicant and team are competent to carry out the project as described

- Include references that show how the team has already answered related questions or used similar methods to answer different questions
- List any involvement in funded research projects.
- List other project management, experience or training if you are an early career researcher and this is your first grant.
- Ensure that the research teams' publications demonstrate an ability to use all the research methods necessary for the project.

Two possible additional propositions, concerned with project outputs and research environment, are listed below.

### Additional proposition: project outputs will be relevant to non-academic beneficiaries

- Provide a list of anticipated publications with evidence that you are likely to achieve them (e.g. previous track record, publishing contracts).
- Demonstrate why each piece of dissemination is likely to be effective in communicating with the target audience.
- If your project includes non-academic outputs such as websites, exhibitions or user events, provide a detailed description of each with concrete information on likely costs, number of participants, duration, location etc., that show each is achievable.
- Show that each team member has a range of tasks suitable to their seniority and time allocated to the project.

### Additional proposition: the institution is likely to support the research team appropriately

- List any non-standard resources that the host institution and any partners will provide (e.g. laboratories, research equipment, research time, statistical advice, training, research governance services, computing equipment, access to participants, etc.).
- Calculate any financial or 'in kind' commitments made by the host institution (e.g. staff time, match funding, equipment). The more you can include the better. Note that resources purchased by other research grants still 'belong' to the institution and that you can include them in your calculations for future applications.
- If appropriate, detail any mentoring arrangements or steering groups provided from within the institution.

This process will leave you with a quantity of raw evidence that you can then order and link to create a compelling argument. Use the funding agency guidance and Appendix 2 to decide which piece of information fits into which section of the application template.

---

TOOL 14

# ARGUMENTS AND EVIDENCE: THE 10 STEP PROCESS

This Tool helps you develop the arguments and evidence that will form the building blocks of your research grant application. If you follow these steps, you are unlikely to become so overwhelmed by the technical challenges of grant-writing that you fail to make your application convincing to referees and non-specialist grants' committee members:

1 Read the agency guidance for both applicants and assessors.
2 Produce an initial project design and structure using the advice in Chapter 7.
3 Collate evidence to support each proposition using Tool 13 (*Produce Your Evidence*).
4 Identify potential weaknesses or areas for misunderstanding.
5 Collate defensive evidence to refute each of them.
6 Use Appendix 2 to ensure that the four important messages and key propositions are allocated to the appropriate sections of the application document.
7 Ensure consistency across sections of your case for support by breaking down your project into three to five sub-questions or things 'we need to know' plus matching components of research activity.
8 As you write, use the 'chunking' technique to group related items under the same heading and structure your text in the most memorable way.
9 Use applicant and assessor guidance to check that no evidence is missing.
10 Test your draft application (see Chapter 11).

# TEN

## HOW TO WRITE FOR FUNDING AGENCIES: LANGUAGE AND STYLE

## Summary

This chapter explains how to write research grant applications that stand out against the competition. It provides a set of writing techniques that help make your research grant applications easy to read, easy to understand and convincing. The examples given throughout this chapter are taken from a series of successful grant applications, which illustrate some of the advice and guidance. You can find more information about each of these in Appendix 3.

## Introduction

Well-written applications perform three functions for the referees and grants' committees who decide whether projects deserve funding. In brief, they must be:

1  Easy to read
2  Easy to understand
3  Convincing

These qualities are important success factors in tough research funding competitions.

It is perfectly acceptable for a grants' committee member to say, 'This one was so badly written that I could not work out what they want to do.' However, 'badly written' has a specific meaning in this context.

Unfortunately, researchers who write well for publication may not have impressive grant-writing skills. This is because other forms of academic writing, such as monographs, journal articles or PhD theses, have rather different aims. They are all written for specialist readers, who have the time and inclination to read them carefully.

In contrast, research grant applications are read quickly and the readers are not always specialist in your areas. The funding decision is made by a grants' committee that ranks applications against each other. Your writing style must suit this environment and help your application to stand out against the competition.

This chapter helps improve your grant-writing skills through a set of six core grant-writing techniques plus specific, additional advice on how to make your applications easy to read, easy to understand and convincing.

You do not need to adopt all of these techniques or aim for a bland, clinical writing style. Inevitably, some of them will suit you more than others. As long as you create applications that meet the three objectives, you do not need to follow every single piece of advice in this chapter.

In practice, each of following core writing techniques will help you meet the three writing objectives while refining the structure of your project proposal.

1 *Assert–justify*: how to tell readers the point of an argument before giving the detail of an argument.
2 *Priming*: how to give readers advance information that will make them likely to accept the key arguments and demands.
3 *Signposting*: how to tell readers what information is coming so that they are ready to read important information when it comes.
4 *Linking*: how to create connected arguments across the case for support.
5 *Labelling*: how to demonstrate a consistent and logical project structure.
6 *Summary*: how to create a strong project summary.

# 1   Assert–justify

The 'assert–justify' technique requires you to make an assertion and then justify it with evidence rather than argue your case and then make a conclusion.

This goes against the grain for many researchers, who are versed in a traditional academic 'argue–conclude' model. However, the nuanced and cautious approach of 'argue–conclude' does not suit grant-writing, where the emphasis needs to be on simple, direct communication.

There are three advantages to starting with an assertion and following it with the evidence:

- Speed-readers pick up all the main messages because speed-reading focuses on the bold propositions that begin each section
- Detail-readers are motivated to read on because the bold proposition at the start of each section tells them the purpose of the argument they want to absorb
- The assertions can be lifted out and used to write your summary

'Assert–justify' also has an important structuring function. You can use this technique to order your overall case for support, as well as each section of text and each paragraph. This is because each level of your application has its own internal structure, in which a message is first communicated clearly and then justified with evidence.

---

EXAMPLE 30

---

## THE ULTIMATE 'ASSERT–JUSTIFY'

The next example – taken from a lengthy European funding application – shows an interesting and marked use of the 'assert–justify' technique. Each paragraph of the background section starts with a 'stand-out' assertion in bold, which is backed up by a paragraph of evidence.

**The consortium will build on a strong software development platform.**

The aim of the project is to introduce property-driven development into the software engineering process. Property-driven development can be used in a variety of programming languages and systems. The particular platform chosen for initial implementation of the project is Erlang/OTP (Open Telecom Platform), but a crucial aspect of our proposal is the dissemination and adoption of the approach much more widely, particularly into the model driven development arena (UML) and other implementation languages (C/C++, Java, etc.). Erlang/OTP has been chosen as the implementation vehicle because of its robustness and reliability within the telecoms sector; witness, for example, its success in the implementation of the AXD301 ATM telecoms switch by Ericsson, one of the project partners. Erlang is a practical language, designed from the start with practical application in mind. It also benefits from simplicity, and from being a functional language, which eases the application of theoretical results from the academic programming language community. We see Erlang as a natural common ground between researchers and the telecoms industry, providing a conduit through which research results can be quickly transferred to industrial applications, and hence into a wider industrial context. We see precisely this happening in this project. *Software Testing European Project*

This is an effective way of helping speed-readers navigate an application document that is over 100 pages long.

# 2 Priming: key arguments and demands

Priming is how you influence readers' reactions to key arguments by feeding them contextual information in advance. It is the single most important way that a research grant application builds enthusiasm among readers.

Have you noticed that two miles before every motorway service station there is a sign warning about driving while tired? Priming is widely studied by cognitive psychologists, and widely used as a sales technique. For example, you are more likely to buy an insurance policy if you feel worried about the likely disasters beforehand. An insurance company will make sure you feel these concerns before starting the sales pitch.

In brief, priming is about giving the reader the evidence that will make them likely to agree with your main propositions. Instead of describing your project as 'important' or 'exciting', you give the readers relevant information in advance and allow them to form their own judgements. By the time they reach the principal statement and discussion of your main propositions they will be easy to convince.

As you write, you should concentrate on priming your four key propositions, as follows:

## The importance proposition: this proposal asks an important question

Use the 'we have a problem' section (however labelled by the funding agency) to feed readers with information that makes them worried that we do not know the answer, or excited that we could know the answer to your question. This primes them so that when they read the full statement of your research question and details of the activity that answers it, they are ready to support your demands.

 **EXAMPLE 31A**

### PRIMING AN IMPORTANT QUESTION

This example primes the applicants' main research question on how the extraordinary rendition and proxy detention of terror suspects has developed and whether they are US-led phenomena. In the second paragraph of the case for support, they state the number of individuals affected and provide evidence for rendition and detention as widespread practices. This primes the 'need to know' message of the research sub-questions later in the document.

US Congress provided a sense of the intensity of US involvement in the system of rendition and proxy detention in August 2006 when it reported that 14,000 people were being held without due process in secret locations by the security agencies of dozens of states worldwide, on behalf of the US (Quinn 2006). The current US administration continues to operate under authorisation granted by Congress in 2001 to use force against Al Qaida suspects anywhere in the world, force which includes indefinite detention by the US or its allies without due process (Roth 2010). *Rendition and Detention Project*

## The success proposition: this project is likely to answer the question

The 'we have a problem' section of your case for support is also crucial to priming the likely success of your project. In this section, you introduce the list of things you 'need to know'. In providing evidence for why we 'need to know' the answers to your questions, you prime the plan of investigation.

When readers reach the detailed account of your research activity later in the case for support, they will be easier to convince. They should already agree that we 'need to know' answers to your questions and that your approach is likely to provide these answers.

### EXAMPLE 31B

## PRIMING THE PROBLEM

A further extract from the same funded application uses the Background section to prime three regional case studies that form the basis of the proposed research programme:

> Despite the widespread and well established use of rendition, scholarly work has tended to focus on its status in law (Parry 2005; Weissbrodt and Bergquist 2006; Sadat 2007). There has been no work to examine how the system has emerged and how it operates. Early evidence suggests that the operation of rendition and proxy detention may be much more diffuse. It also appears to be operating differently in the three regions most involved (Asia, the Middle East and Africa) (Cageprisoners 2006a). *Rendition and Detention Project*

## The value proposition: the likely gain from this project is worth the resources requested

Use the 'this project is the solution' section (however labelled by the funding agency) to prime readers about your budget and justification of costs. As you describe each activity component in detail, make sure you mention all relevant project resources.

If you weave every budget item into the case for support narrative, decision makers are more likely to agree that the grant requested is necessary and sufficient.

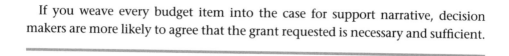

## PRIMING THE RESOURCES

In this extract, the applicants use the 'Research Methods' section of their case for support to argue for the efficiency of conducting the research in person:

> Funding is sought for the PI and Co-I to undertake the research because we will need to be immersed in the issues with a detailed understanding of the background to each case before writing up the research findings, particularly as each case will be informed by disparate sources, and the material concerns sensitive subjects. The PI will work on Pakistan and Syria, since she has already undertaken some pilot work on these cases, and the Co-I will work on Kenya, as he has experience of analysing US foreign policy in Africa since 9/11 (Stokes and Raphael 2010). Both scholars are well versed in the foreign policy practices of the US, and in analysing security collaborations between the US and its allies, including in relation to the use of violence. This equips us well to analyse the data efficiently, which will help ensure the research is completed in a timely way, and while the issue is still current. *Rendition and Detention Project*

### The competence proposition: the applicant and team are competent to carry out the project as described

Self-citation in the 'we have a problem' section is a way of priming readers to believe that your contribution to the field has been important and is likely to be so again. They can then turn to your CV or 'Track Record' section for a full account of your achievements.

## PRIMING THE INVESTIGATORS

In this extract, the early career applicants (i.e. Blakeley and Raphael) use a section of text on project outputs to showcase their previous contribution to the three fields relevant to their project:

> The research will contribute to debates in International Relations in three areas:
>
> 1  **Security Collaborations**: it will contribute to our understanding of security collaborations that bring together security agencies from multiple states. In this regard the work builds on earlier work of the PI (Blakeley 2006, 2007, 2009) and of the Co-I (Raphael 2010).

2 **Critical Terrorism Studies**: it will contribute to the growing body of work on state terrorism, understood as the use or threat of violence by agents of the state to instil fear in an audience beyond direct victims, so that they are forced to change their behaviour in some way (Blakeley 2009: 30). Families and peers of those subjected to rendition are likely to suffer extreme fear about the fate of the disappeared, as well as the terror of themselves being subjected to rendition. Thus, it can be argued that rendition has a terrorising effect.

3 **Security Studies**: the research will contribute to theory building in Security Studies. As discussed below, three alternative models – the hierarchical model, the co-option model, and the diffusion model – have been identified by the PI to help explain how rendition and proxy detention have emerged and are operating. These three models, as well as their application in this research, will provide a helpful framework for further work in the Security Studies field on a variety of collaborative arrangements between security agencies that transcend state boundaries. *Rendition and Detention Project*

# 3   Signposting important information

Signposting is much more explicit than priming. Priming feeds the reader information in order to create a state of mind that will make them more likely to be convinced by a future argument. Signposting prepares the reader to process important information by telling them that the information is coming.

This technique allows readers to stay alongside your arguments. It tells speed-readers when they can safely skip a block of text and, more importantly, tells detail-readers when they need to pay close attention.

As with 'assert–justify', signposting can be used at various levels of your application document. For example, the 'Introduction' to your case for support or 'Background' section should be used to briefly state the overall research question, why it is important and a short summary of the project and its aims. Equally, as you take the reader into each new section, you should introduce your argument with a signpost sentence.

━━━━━━━━━━━━━━━━━━━━ EXAMPLE 32 ━━━━━━━━━━━━━━━━━━━━

### SECTION SIGNPOSTS

This extract uses two straightforward signposts within one paragraph (in italics):

Existing work by consortium members is at the forefront of automated testing for concurrent systems, particularly in the telecoms sector. *In this section we describe* how this will be carried forward and broadened by the project, extending the state of the art in testing evolving systems, in monitoring system behaviour

THE RESEARCH FUNDING TOOLKIT

and in verification of concurrent systems. *We now set out the state of the art* in these areas, and explain how the project will deliver progress in all of them. *Software Testing European Project*

In contrast, this signpost uses a summary of the section content to introduce the 'Research Methods' section:

These five behavioural experiments assess the impact of reconsolidation on the acquisition of words by capitalising on either the phonetic or meaning similarities between the reactivated and to-be-learnt competing knowledge. *Memory Research Project*

---

## 4 Linking: creating connected arguments

Linking is a technique that helps connect your arguments throughout the entire case for support narrative.

Funding agencies sometimes prescribe an elaborate structure and set of headings for the case for support. The effort of following this guidance correctly can mean that the overall narrative becomes disconnected.

As a result, referees and grants' committee members are left to make their own connections between your background, research questions, methods and research programme sections.

Leaving your readers to their own devices in this way is risky. On the one hand, they may make the wrong connections. On the other, busy referees and grants' committee members may find no connections and consider your project disorganised. Providing your own connections between different sections of your case for support is the safer route.

Linking helps you carry forward the key message of the previous section and show how it informs the argument of the next. If you link your case for support effectively, decision makers will finish reading with a clearer sense of all four key propositions.

Consequently, your ability to 'link' your project effectively is a good test of your project design and structure. This is because good links are dependent on all the various elements contributing to the overall design and structure.

 EXAMPLE 33

### LINKING COMPONENTS

This brief extract from a successful application shows the relationship between the outcome of one project component (an experiment that measures pain) and the next experiment in the series:

---

This will provide some practically useful behavioural measures related to pain, and so will help to refine endpoint estimates. However, these results may not necessarily inform on the animals' subjective perception and overall pain experience. This will be measured in approach 2. *Research Animal Project*

This link is particularly effective because it shows how the two experiments inform each other while demonstrating that the second is not dependent on the outcome of the first.

## 5  Labelling: consistent and logical structure

As discussed in Chapter 7, a well-designed project breaks down its overall research question into three to five things we 'need to know', which each match a project objective and component of research activity.

An important writing task is to emphasise this consistent structure by highlighting the themes that run across the application document.

The best way to do this is with a series of identical sub-headings and repeated phrases ('tag phrases'). These should be used consistently throughout the case for support to label each theme and show the connection between research sub-question, objective and component of activity. These labels make your text easier to understand while convincing decision makers that your project is well designed.

'Tag phrases' are also useful in relation to key technical terms or theoretical concepts that might challenge non-specialist readers. The repeated and consistent use of a complex phrase helps readers feel that they understand it. You should also use 'tag phrases' to label shorter pieces of text, such as individual research questions.

EXAMPLE 34

### TAG PHRASES

The following list of examples shows how 'tag phrases' are used in practice by some of the funded applications in this book:

1  The *Detention and Rendition Project* uses 'hierarchical', 'co-option' and 'diffusion' as labels for three theoretical models and these can be found in the research questions, summary, background and methods section of the case for support. This gives the project logic and structure and helps the reader perceive the project as well organised and planned.

2  In the *Memory Research Project* the applicant uses several longer 'tag phrases' repeatedly and in prominent parts of the application document. This approach helps readers understand the project and the grants' committee members to formulate supportive presentations. The 'tag phrases' include 'traditional views of learning assume that new memories remain shaky for a short period', 'this project bridges the gap between animal neuroscience and psycholinguistics' and 'revising established knowledge shortly before learning similar information is ill-advised'. These are three important messages for anyone reading this project proposal.

3  In the *Research Animal Project* the applicants use versions of the following three phrases repeatedly throughout the case for support: 'humane endpoint', 'welfare assessment' and 'arbitrary guidelines'. The three tag phrases encapsulate the central argument of the project: 'arbitrary guidelines' mean that current 'welfare assessment' of laboratory mice do not necessarily result in 'humane endpoints'. This ensures that even the most casual speed-readers, such as the wider grants' committee, understand the main messages of the application.

# 6   High-impact summary

The first section of a research grant application that all referees and grants' committee members turn to is the 'Summary', 'Abstract' or 'Project Outline'. If you fail to gain readers' interest here, you are unlikely to succeed elsewhere in your document. Your summary has an essential role in making your project stand out against others in the same competition.

In addition, it may be the only part that the wider grants' committee reads properly. A well-written summary will make them believe they have read and understood your application. It will also help the designated member formulate their presentation at the committee meeting.

The summary provides a preview of your entire project in simple language. Like a news story, it should be both factual and compelling. In order to write a strong summary:

* Avoid adjectives or adverbs that do not provide factual information.
* Make no claims that your project is exciting or important – allow the evidence to speak for itself.
* Lead with either the research question (if it is easy to explain its importance) or the need that the research question will fill (if this is not obvious).
* Only use vocabulary that you would find in a quality national newspaper. Either place essential technical terms in inverted commas at this stage (and define them) or just use the definition and introduce the technical terms later in the document.

As well as providing an overview of the question, activity and outputs, the summary is crucial to helping readers to understand your project. It starts the process that enables them to grasp the research question, to appreciate its importance and to understand how it will be solved by different parts of the research project. Although the summary opens your case for support, you should write it last and craft it carefully.

This does not mean it should be written in isolation. An application that is written using the 'assert–justify' approach will provide key sentences that you can transpose into your summary.

Some funding agencies provide a dedicated section of the application form for your project summary. This means that the case for support template may start with a different heading, such as 'Track Record', 'Introduction' or 'Aims'. Whatever the agency guidance, you should always open your case for support with some form of summary. The following examples from successful applications illustrate this.

---

**EXAMPLE 35**

## CASE FOR SUPPORT SUMMARY

In the first example, the funding agency template requires a 'Research Track Record' section followed by 'Background'. In both cases, the applicants manage to include summary text in the opening lines:

1   Research Track Record

   We propose a collaboration between the Natural Language Generation Group of the Department of Computing at the Open University, and the BioHealth Informatics Group in the School of Computer Science at the University of Manchester, with the aim of developing a reliable Natural Language interface through which ontology builders and other users can encode metadata on the Semantic Web...

2   Background

   We seek a set of principles by which logic-based descriptions (especially ontologies on the Semantic Web) can be associated with transparent formulations in natural languages. By applying these principles, we will demonstrate a tool that allows subject-matter experts to edit and query metadata on the Semantic Web through a reliable Natural Language interface. *Web Authoring Project*

The second example uses a template with an opening section entitled 'Specific Aims'. The applicant starts this section with a straightforward project summary.

Specific Aims

Understanding language is one of the most fundamental human cognitive abilities. It plays an important role in normal development, and is the major means for acquiring information in many domains. A number of psychological disorders (e.g., schizophrenia) can disrupt the normally impressive functioning of this system, greatly exacerbating the negative consequences of these disorders.

Psycholinguists have made significant progress in clarifying the structures and processes that underlie language comprehension. Despite this progress, much remains to be learned about how words are represented in a person's 'mental lexicon'. Critical remaining issues in this area revolve around questions of lexical representation, and lexical access. Theories must specify how the presentation of a spoken word leads to a particular lexical representation becoming activated, and what the effects of such activation are: What effect does one active lexical representation have on others, and on units at other levels of representation?

The current proposal includes a large set of theoretically-driven empirical studies of lexical activation. The experiments use a range of different methodologies, in order to assure correct theoretical inferences through converging operations. The empirical investigations are organized into three interlocking groups of experiments. *Spoken Word Project*

In both cases the applicants appreciate the need to gain the readers' interest in the opening lines of their case for support as well as follow the agency guidance.

You can read all of the summaries from the successful applications used in this section in Appendix 3.

---

# The easy-to-read application

Adopting the core techniques (especially *Assert–justify*, *Linking* and *Labelling*) goes a long way towards creating 'easy-to-read' grant applications. However, the following simple writing techniques will also help referees and grants' committee members read your application with fluency.

## 1 Use adjectives sparingly

Multiple adjectives may add flourish but they do make your text harder to read and understand. Try to stick to one adjective and only use them when necessary to your meaning. They slow the reader down and make them process several words in order to grasp one concept. In addition, only use adjectives that provide a factual qualification of the noun. Avoid adjectives like 'exciting', 'significant' or 'profound'. If you want your readers to find your project 'exciting', then you need to provide evidence rather than adjectives.

## 2 Use adverbs even more sparingly

Use adverbs even more sparingly than adjectives. It is better to use the right verb.

## 3 Do not use typography to emphasise too much text

Do not use typographical features (bold, underlining, italics) too often within blocks of text. Information that is this important must always come at the start of a paragraph and needs no further emphasis. It is irritating to read blocks of text that include too many typographical variations.

## 4 Use bullet points and numbered lists for multiple examples or concepts

If you need to list three or more examples, elements, events or reasons, use a numbered list or bullet points. This shows the reader that the piece of text is to be read differently from a paragraph that develops an argument.

## 5 Keep your paragraphs short

Use short paragraphs – try to make six lines your maximum. Anything longer becomes harder for the reader to follow and means that they are liable to skip information. You may feel that you need longer paragraphs in order to squeeze more information into your case for support. This is a false economy. You may squeeze more information in but the reader is less likely to understand or remember it.

## 6 Keep your paragraph structure simple

Front load the key information to the first sentence of each paragraph rather than building up to it. Do not bury important messages halfway through a paragraph so that they can only be found after careful re-reading. Use the rest of the paragraph to explain your important messages. This also makes your application easier to understand.

## 7 Use simple punctuation

Avoid colons and semi-colons as far as possible. They are usually a sign that your sentences are too long. Use every punctuation mark as opportunity to split a long sentence into two short ones.

## 8 Keep your sentences short

Keep your sentences short. They are easier to read, especially for busy referees and grants' committee members. If you use lots of complex sentences, your readers are unlikely to understand them after one reading. As a rule, sentences that include more than 20 words are too long. Ten-word sentences are ideal. Long sentences should be rare.

## 9 Keep your verb structures simple

Try to use the present tense in its active form. As you revise your application document, take time to simplify the verb structure. This will save on word count and makes your application easier to read and understand.

For example, 'this project asks' can replace any of the following:

This project will ask...

The question to be asked by this project is...

This project is asking the following question...

It is expected that the project will ask...

# The easy-to-understand application

If your application is easy to read, then it is halfway to being easy to understand. The core techniques (especially *Signposting*, *Labelling* and the *High-impact summary*) also help ensure that referees and grants' committee members understand your research design, project structure and follow your arguments.

In addition, you may find that the following simple writing techniques prevent readers from becoming confused or lost as they work through your applications.

## 1 Avoid new or specialist acronyms

Unless an acronym is in common use and comprehensible to everyone within your wider research field, spell it out in full. Frequency of use within your discipline or field is not sufficient justification for including it in a research grant application. Spelling a phrase in full on first use (with the acronym in brackets) is not enough. Referees and grants' committee members do not have time to pause and remember the significance of your acronyms. If you employ acronyms because you do not have enough space, you have written too much. Some research communities like to use slightly jokey acronyms as short versions of their project titles and there is no real harm in this.

## 2 Avoid new or specialist abbreviations

As with acronyms, do not coin abbreviations to save space. If you run out of space you need to edit out whole sentences and paragraphs, not condense your text. Unfamiliar abbreviations confuse, irritate and bore readers in the same way as unfamiliar acronyms.

## 3 Define technical terms and use them consistently

Technical terms are sometimes unavoidable, especially for scientists. If there is no everyday synonym you will have to use them. When you introduce a technical term to your application document, provide a clear definition in everyday terms. Ensure that you then use the phrase consistently (and in full) so that it becomes familiar to your non-specialist readers. Consider making it a tag phrase. Do not tax their memory or understanding by using abbreviations.

## 4 Avoid within-discipline jargon

Technical terms sometimes have their place in research grant applications but within-discipline jargon is always confusing, irritating and boring. However, applicants often get a sense of security from using jargon. You may even find it hard to tell whether you are using it in the first place. Once you identify the offending words or phrases, provide simple synonyms (e.g. 'gap' for 'lacuna').

## 5 Repetition is good

In the context of a research grant application, repetition is good. Word count restrictions and the impossibility of saying everything you want to about your project will prevent endless repetition. However, communicating with busy, non-specialist readers means that you should repeat key information at more than one point in your application document. You should also convert essential technical terms into repeated 'tag phrases' (see *Labelling*).

## 6 Avoid synonyms (because repetition is good)

If you need to refer to the same thing more than once, use the same word or phrase throughout the application. If you use a different word or phrase at later points, you will confuse the reader. Using a different word sends the signal that you mean something different. The speed-reader must understand what you mean instantly.

You may feel that your writing becomes dull if you do not introduce some variation. However, elegant variations make your text harder to understand. Either use a direct repetition to reinforce your message or edit it out.

## 7 Use descriptive titles

Do not rely on numbers to describe the activity in your research programme. Use something that is descriptive of the content (see *Labelling* earlier in this chapter for more information). 'Research Question 1', 'Experiment 1', 'Phase 1' and 'Study 1' are harder to remember than descriptive labels.

## 8 Use natural syntax

Try reading a draft of your application out loud. Can you do this easily? Or do you use elaborate sentences and vocabulary? If your application is hard to read in this way, referees and grants' committee members will also find it hard to understand.

# The convincing application

The *Priming* and *High-impact summary* core techniques are especially effective in convincing readers that your project deserves funding. If you have followed the advice in previous chapters and structured your case for support well, with plenty of impressive evidence to back up your arguments, your application will already look convincing.

There are two additional points to bear in mind.

## 1 Avoid hyperbole – show rather than tell

The minute you start describing your project as 'enormously significant' or 'exceptional' you raise doubts in the minds of the reader. While you will need to guide them through your argument, you need to give them evidence rather than quality judgements. They will not judge your project 'exceptional' just because you describe it in those terms.

## 2 Check your grammar and spelling

Spelling mistakes (such as 'principle investigator') or typographical errors are not acceptable and make your application less convincing. However, journalistic conventions are preferable to pedantic attention to correct grammar. Quality national newspapers often publish style guides and these are useful reference points for research grant applicants.

## Conclusion

After reading this chapter, you should have a set of effective grant-writing techniques. These will help you create applications that are easy to read, easy to understand and convincing. The next chapter shows you how to test your draft applications and work out whether they are ready to submit.

# ELEVEN

## HOW TO TEST YOUR DRAFT APPLICATIONS

### Summary

This chapter looks at how to get valid feedback on your draft applications in order to improve your chances of winning a grant. As well as describing how and when to seek feedback, it discusses the categories of colleague and associate best qualified to help you.

You may also like to read Appendix 1, which describes a set of useful workshop activities. Meanwhile, this chapter focuses on tests that you can easily organise yourself without help from administrators or your institution.

There are 12 Tests in this chapter. Each is appropriate to a particular stage in the development process and helps assess a specific element of your research grant application.

| Test | Purpose |
| --- | --- |
| 1 Reality Check Test | Whether you and your project are right for the target scheme |
| 2 Project Design Test 1 | Whether your project design is sound |
| 3 Project Design Test 2 | Whether your project design is sound |
| 4 Readability Test | Whether your application is easy for a busy person to read |
| 5 Easy-to-Understand Test | Whether your application is easy for a non-specialist to understand |
| 6 Blueprint Test | Whether your application includes enough information about how you will carry out the research |
| 7 Memory Test | Whether your application is clearly structured, labelled and memorable |
| 8 Propositions Test | Whether you make and justify the key propositions needed to convince decision makers |
| 9 Rejection Test | How to predict referees' comments |
| 10 Speed-Read Test | Whether your application suits the needs of speed-readers |
| 11 Review Panel | How to test your application under grants' committee conditions |
| 12 Referee Report Test | How to read and understand feedback on rejected applications |

# Introduction

This chapter provides a series of tests that you can apply to check whether your research grant applications are well designed, suitable for the target funding scheme, easy to speed-read, easy to understand and convincing.

Each test is designed to highlight the potential flaws that will be exposed by the funding decision agency decision-making process, which is described in Chapter 5.

Each exercise has a recommendation for a suitable 'tester'. This is because getting reliable feedback is easier if the 'tester' has the right experience and perspective. However, this chapter recognises that you may not always have access to grants' committee members and regular funding agency referees.

Most of the tests are designed so that less experienced colleagues can carry them out with less possibility of misguided and unhelpful feedback.

# Why test?

You need to test your draft applications in order to show up flaws that will become apparent during the evaluation process. Encouragement and supportive comments are damaging in this context as they have no bearing on the eventual outcome and give you false hope.

As the author, you will find it hard to spot those flaws that may lose you the grant. This is because you are an expert in your area and spent a long period designing your project and creating the application document.

In contrast, your application document is evaluated quickly by a group of academics who are unfamiliar with your research area. They have limited time to read and understand the nuances of your project. In addition, they do not approach your research with natural enthusiasm.

As a result, you are not well qualified to check whether your own research grant applications are easy to read, easy to understand and convincing. You can only achieve this by asking someone else to read them. In order to get good feedback, you must ensure that your testers take a non-specialist perspective and are prepared to be critical.

# What to test

As discussed throughout this book, there are three things that make research grant applications fundable:

- They are easy for non-specialists to understand
- They are easy for busy non-specialists to speed-read
- They convince critical, busy non-specialists

In order to meet these three criteria you must produce an important, well-designed, achievable project that represents value for money to the funding agency. The project must be described in an application document that meets the agency criteria and contains convincing arguments and evidence. All the information must be presented as clearly and simply as possible in order to help the decision makers do their job properly.

In order to test a draft application properly, the conditions of funding agency evaluation must be replicated. If your available pool of 'testers' has grants' committee and referee experience, you have a head start. If you do not have this sort of access, there are alternatives as long as you test with care.

## Who should test?

The qualities that disqualify Principal Investigators as reliable judges of their own research grant applications also apply to trusted collaborators. This group has the following drawbacks as a source of valid criticism:

- They are expert in the area and understand your methods and terminology
- They are sympathetic to the area and will defend it against competing areas
- They do not necessarily understand the grant-giving process and may not have acted as referees or grants' committee members
- They may be unwilling to make negative comments as they fear hurting your feelings or making you angry

This means that you should avoid obtaining feedback from this group unless it is under very controlled conditions. Expert collaborators can be very useful in helping you test your design and methods but should take a more limited role in relation to draft applications.

In general, academic colleagues from other fields with extensive grants' committee and referee experience make the best types of 'tester'. There are even some tests which are most usefully carried out by non-academic associates. Each test in this chapter recommends the most suitable 'tester' and specifies any group to avoid.

In an ideal world, you should draw on the following pool of colleagues and associates as regular 'testers':

- Academic colleagues with a good publication record from outside your immediate discipline
- Research administrators and other literate non-academics with a decent level of general education
- Grants' committee members
- Regular reviewers for target funding schemes
- Consistently and recently successful applicants to your target funding agency
- Students, research assistants and research associates

However, you may not have access to these groups (though you should ask yourself what is wrong with your institution or personal network if you do not). Even if you do, researchers who are busy running large funded projects or in senior management roles may not have much time to spare.

Consequently, some of these tests have been designed to get very specific feedback from any research-active academic colleague with a good publication record and common sense. As long as your 'tester' follows the instructions to the letter, valid feedback should ensue.

This is because each test is designed to make every 'tester' respond in the same way as non-specialist referees and grants' committee members. It may even be that you and close colleagues can learn to step out of your supportive and expert collaborator roles when it comes to providing grant application feedback. If you achieve this, you have the makings of a very powerful and immediately accessible support group. However, unstructured feedback from close colleagues with little personal experience of awarding grants should always be interpreted for what it is.

## How to test

This chapter provides 12 different tests you can apply to your draft application at various stages in the development process. Each is designed to test a different aspect of your proposed project or application document.

You should try to use as many of these tests as possible. Each test has a different objective and the instructions for each include a recommendation on who you should invite to carry out the test and at what stage in the application process you should use it. Many only take a few minutes to conduct.

In practice, your working environment, access to the right people and ability to share your ideas might limit the number of tests that you actually use. However, you should always try to test the following aspects of your draft:

1  Suitability of project for the target funding agency
2  Project design and methods

---

· THE RESEARCH FUNDING TOOLKIT

3 Evidence and arguments

4 Writing and presentation

Only when you have checked that all aspects of your application document are as strong as possible should you go ahead and submit your grant proposal. Remember: the pain of rigorous testing is less than the pain of rejection.

# The tests

The following tests have been tightly specified in order to get the right sort of feedback on your application. Each one is appropriate for a different stage in the application process.

**TEST TIMETABLE**

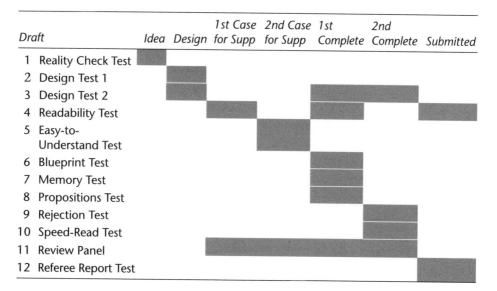

| Draft | Idea | Design | 1st Case for Supp | 2nd Case for Supp | 1st Complete | 2nd Complete | Submitted |
|---|---|---|---|---|---|---|---|
| 1 Reality Check Test | ■ | | | | | | |
| 2 Design Test 1 | | ■ | | | | | |
| 3 Design Test 2 | | ■ | | | ■ | ■ | |
| 4 Readability Test | | | ■ | ■ | ■ | | ■ |
| 5 Easy-to-Understand Test | | | | ■ | | | |
| 6 Blueprint Test | | | | | ■ | | |
| 7 Memory Test | | | | | ■ | | |
| 8 Propositions Test | | | | | ■ | | |
| 9 Rejection Test | | | | | | ■ | |
| 10 Speed-Read Test | | | | | | ■ | |
| 11 Review Panel | | ■ | ■ | ■ | ■ | | |
| 12 Referee Report Test | | | | | | | ■ |

You can carry out the *Readability* test on your own because its criteria are completely objective. The other tests need input from various categories of colleagues and associates. Some tests work on an individual level and others involve small groups working together on one application. None of the group tests takes very long so they can be used by a group of colleagues working on a batch of grant applications.

The *Review Panel* test requires a group of applicants to work together and has also been included in Appendix 1 as it may require more organisational and institutional support.

# *1* Reality check test

*Purpose*: To check whether you are targeting the right funding scheme and have the right overall application strategy

*Timing*: When you have both a research idea and a target funding scheme

*Testers*: You and an academic colleague with a funding success track record and/or an experienced research administrator

## Assemble the following information:

- Your research idea and a rough list of the types of resources you will need (staff, equipment, travel, investigator time)
- The relevant evaluation and eligibility criteria for the scheme from the funding agency's website
- The relevant referee and grants' committee report forms and guidance (if published)
- A list of eligible and ineligible costs for the scheme from the funding agency's website
- A list of previously funded projects by the same scheme
- Any information that the funding agency publishes on how it chooses referees and its peer review college or membership of its committees
- The scheme success rates (usually available from the website and/or the funding agency's annual report)

## Using this information, ask the following questions:

- Does my project sit comfortably within the range of projects typically funded by this scheme (in terms of topic, discipline, scope, etc.)?
- Are the resources I need allowed by the scheme?
- What will I do with the idea if it is rejected by this funding agency?
- What sort of person is likely to make the decision about my application?
- What do I need to include in the application document in order to ensure a positive report by the likely decision makers?
- Are the resources similar in type and quantity to those obtained by other applicants to the scheme?

## Use your answers to:

- Decide whether your proposed project is right for the funding scheme
- Decide whether your proposed project requests the right level of resources (too little is as damaging as too much)
- Plan convincing arguments for your draft application
- Decide how to recycle or develop your idea if your application is rejected

THE RESEARCH FUNDING TOOLKIT

## 2   Project design test 1

*Purpose*:  To test your project design
*Timing*:  When you have a basic plan of your project and methods but before you start writing your application
*Testers*:  Colleagues who work in a similar area and whose judgement you trust

Invite a group of colleagues who work in the same area or with similar methods to a 30-minute meeting in a room equipped with a white board. Give yourself 10 minutes to explain the project to them and then take questions. Brief them not to make quality judgements but to interrogate your rationale and project design.

Use this feedback to refine your project design or to decide how to defend it when you write your application.

## 3   Project design test 2

*Purpose*:  To test your project design
*Timing*:  When you have written an outline of your project and methods but before you start writing your application document
*Testers*:  Colleagues from the same research group, laboratory or department

Prepare a one-page summary of your project and book a short lunchtime meeting with colleagues from the same research group or laboratory. Allow them 30 minutes to read your summary while they eat their sandwiches and then take questions for a further 30 minutes. Brief them not to make quality judgements but to interrogate your rationale and project design.

Use this feedback to refine your project design or decide how to defend it when you write your application.

## 4   Readability test

*Purpose*:  To test whether your text is easy to read
*Timing*:  First draft of case for support and first complete draft stages
*Testers*:  You can do this yourself or persuade a non-academic friend, colleague or family member to help

Check your draft, as follows:

- Is every sentence less than 20 words long?
- Is your average paragraph less than 6 lines long?
- Is there a line break between each paragraph?
- Is there a double-line break between each section of your case for support?
- Is each printed page of your case for support broken up with two or more of the following:
  - headings?
  - lists (using either numbers or bullet points)?
  - graphs, illustrations or figures?
- Within the case for support as a whole, do you:
  - follow the funding agency's guidance regarding headings?
  - order every heading and subheading using a clear typographical hierarchy?
  - avoid over-using italics, underlining or bold within the body of the text?
- Do you follow the funding agency's guidance regarding font, font size, layout and margins?
- Is your first draft within the specified word count/page limit?

Use this information to produce your second draft.


## 5 Easy-to-understand test

*Purpose*: To test whether an early draft of your application is easy for a non-specialist to understand

*Timing*: Second draft of case for support

*Testers*: Academic colleague from a different field who does not use the same approach or methods

Give your draft application and a highlighter pen to a colleague from the same department but from a different branch of your discipline. Ask them to read it as quickly as possible and mark every word, phrase and sentence that they cannot define. They should pay special attention to within-discipline jargon, technical terms and acronyms.

Use the marked copy as guidance on where you need to provide definitions or use simpler terminology in your next draft.


## 6 Blueprint test

*Purpose*: To test whether you have included sufficient detail about the conduct of your project

*Timing*: First complete draft stage

*Testers*:  Academic colleagues or PhD students who understand your approach and methods but are unfamiliar with your proposed project

Give your draft application to your nominated testers. Ask them to read it carefully as though they were obliged to take over as Principal Investigator and conduct the project successfully and according to your wishes. Tell them that they would have to do this using the instructions in your application document alone.

When they have finished reading, ask them to give you a list of the additional information they need to run the project themselves. If they do not need any further information, ask them to tell you if there is any part of your approach they would change.

Use this feedback to refine your design, adding any extra information and detail about how you propose to conduct your project.

# 7   Memory test

*Purpose*:  To test whether your application is clearly structured, labelled and memorable
*Timing*:  First complete draft stage
*Testers*:  Academic colleagues or PhD students who understand your approach and methods but are unfamiliar with your proposed project

Ask your tester to read the application and tell them that you will ask them some questions about it afterwards that they must try to answer from memory. But don't tell them in advance what the questions will be.

The questions are:

- What is the research question of this project?
- What are the things 'we need to know' in order to answer the question?
- What are the main pieces of activity that tell us the answers to the things 'we need to know?'
- Are there any words or phrases that you remember reading and that seem important to understanding this project?

If your tester can answer these questions, then your project is logical, clearly labelled and well structured.

# 8   Propositions test

*Purpose*:  To test whether your application document is convincing
*Timing*:  First complete draft
*Testers*:  Academic colleagues from outside your immediate field who do not use the same approach and methods

Ask a colleague to read your application and identify evidence that would convince sceptical decision makers that each of the following is true:

1  This proposal asks an important question.
2  This project is likely to answer the question.
3  The likely gain from this project is worth the resources requested.
4  The applicant and team are competent to carry out the project as described.

If you have identified other propositions, you need to make them relate to the funding agency's criteria or the nature of your research, and add them to this list.

After they have completed this exercise, ask yourself the following questions:

• Have they identified the best piece of evidence for each proposition?
• If they have, is the evidence strong enough?

Ask the reader which propositions are least well supported and what extra evidence might make the propositions more convincing.

Use this feedback to revise your project design or the way you present your arguments.

## 9  Rejection test

*Purpose*:  To predict fundamental flaws
*Timing*:  Second complete draft
*Who*:  Academic colleagues, preferably those who review for funding agencies or sit on grants' committees

Give your draft application document to a number of colleagues along with the funding agency guidance for referees. Tell them that they are forced to reject your application and ask them to find:

• Three specific reasons not to fund this application (with evidence)
• Something you could do to make this application quicker and easier to read
• Something you could do to make this application easier to understand

Ask the testers what sort of evidence might convince them that these reasons do not apply.

Use this feedback to incorporate evidence and arguments that refute the criticisms they provide. If the same reasons to reject are suggested by each tester, consider revising your project design. Keep the original feedback on file.

# *10*   Speed-read test

*Purpose*:   To test whether your application is accessible to wider grants' committee members

*Timing*:   Second complete draft stage

*Testers*:   Academic colleagues or PhD students who understand your approach and methods but are unfamiliar with your proposed project

Prepare a version of your case for support in which you delete everything except the summary, the headings and the first line of each paragraph. Alternatively, you could limit the reading time of the entire document to five minutes.

Afterwards, ask the readers:

- What is the research question of this project?
- What are the things 'we need to know' in order to answer the question?
- What are the main pieces of activity that tell us the answers to the things 'we need to know?'

If your tester can answer these questions, then your project is 'speed-readable'.

# *11*   Review panel

*Purpose*:   To replicate some of the conditions of a grants' committee meeting in order to show whether your project is easy to read and easy to understand

*Timing*:   Various (see table on p.139) as agreed with colleagues

*Testers*:   You, three to five fellow applicants, a Chair and a time keeper

This exercise works better if the Chair has grants' committee experience but this is not essential. It takes between 60 and 90 minutes, depending on the number of participants. Each participant must bring two copies of their draft application, which must include a summary. One copy is handed to the Chair on arrival.

The organiser brings enough copies of the template form for each participant (see below).

### Review Panel Test Instructions to Participants

This exercise is not intended to produce quality judgements about the projects we review today. The aim is to find out if these applications are structured and written in a way that helps the designated grants' committee member make a convincing presentation that will excite the rest of the committee.

Please take 15 minutes to read the case for support and extract the following information:

- What does this project ask?
- What is the primary piece of evidence for the:
  - o importance of this question
  - o timeliness of the project

- What are the main research activities that answer the overall question?
- Do they need to do everything they want to do?
- Provide a brief summary of the:
  - o methodological approach
  - o scale of the project
  - o main project expenses

- What is the Principal Investigator's track record in this area?
- What are the main outcomes of the project?

This information will form the basis of a two-minute presentation back to the rest of the panel.

Finally:

Out of 10, how easy was this application to speed-read?

Out of 10, how easily did you find the information requested by these instructions?

The participants sit in a circle and pass their draft application to the person on their left. It helps if you are not sitting next to the person with whom you work most closely. Everyone then has 15 minutes to read the relevant draft and prepare a short presentation using the template. This process feels pressurised and intense so there should be silence throughout to allow colleagues to concentrate.

After 15 minutes, the group reconvenes. Each member of the group gives a two-minute presentation on their allocated application following the template guidance and is not allowed to make any quality judgements. Led by the Chair, the rest of the group then has three minutes to ask questions, to which the presenter alone responds. The applicant must remain silent throughout this process.

At the end of the presentations take some further time to discuss how well represented you felt by the busy non-specialists who took charge of your application and how it felt to work under these conditions. A brief explanation about how this process compares with a 'live' grants' committee by the Chair is also very useful.

## 12   Referee report test

*Purpose*:  To find out why your application was rejected

*Timing*:   As soon as a rejection letter has been received

*Tester*:   You and an academic colleague with a funding success track record and/or an experienced research administrator

Read through all feedback received together with feedback for the Rejection Test, if you have it. Ask yourself the following questions:

- Do any of the criticisms recur or do they all vary?
- Do any of the official reports explicitly state that your project is exciting or important?
- Do the criticisms cluster around any of the following:
  - Design
  - Your track record
  - Resources
  - Methods
  - Dissemination
  - Clarity of expression or amount of evidence provided

Without rejecting any of the criticisms outright, you need to decide which elements of the feedback are valid. These need be accepted and incorporated into any future versions of the project. Deciding that the referee was ignorant, hostile or biased is not relevant to this exercise.

## Conclusion

This chapter suggests a number of ways of testing whether your application is easy to speed-read, easy to understand, convincing to non-specialist decision makers and well designed. When you feel that you have 'passed' the tests, you can submit your application in confidence that it is of a high quality and fit for purpose. Good luck.

# TWELVE

## HOW TO ASSEMBLE YOUR BUDGET

### Summary

This chapter serves a number of purposes. First, it explains how to calculate and present a grant application budget by helping you work out what resources you need, how much of each resource you need and how much each resource should cost. Secondly, it highlights certain factors that prevent you from including particular items in your budget. Thirdly, it addresses the importance of creating a budget that also meets the needs of the host institution and the funding agency.

The two Tools at the end of this chapter will help you do this. The *Is It Worth It?* Tool helps you to decide in advance whether a particular funding agency scheme is financially viable for your type of research. The *Intelligent Questions about Finance* Tool helps you decide whether a particular scheme meets the needs of both the Principal Investigator and the host institution.

### Introduction

When a referee or committee member receives a grant application to assess, the budget total is one of the first things they look at. They will then read the rest of the application with this amount in mind. When they have finished their evaluation, they will decide whether your research question and planned programme of activity is worth the investment requested.

In brief, a research grant application is a demand for money and the way you account for the resources you need and support the *value* proposition is a crucial part of your application document. While a well-constructed and presented budget will not win you the grant, a poor one will certainly wreck your chances. Consequently, you need to spend time and effort on getting your finances right.

However, this is not a simple process, as your budget needs to work on a number of different levels:

1  It must pay you enough to cover for the resources you need.
2  It must meet funding agency rules regarding eligible and ineligible costs.
3  It must represent value for money to the funding agency.
4  The host institution (usually your employer) may expect research grants to generate income beyond the direct expenses of the project.

Consequently, deciding what resources you need and putting a price on them is only one part of your task and resolving such different demands may prove problematic. In some cases, difficulties in creating a workable budget may even force you to abandon a particular research grant application.

It is important to check in advance whether the funding agency or scheme suits both your project and the host institution.

## Cost, price, value and method

In order to produce a budget that meets the needs of the project, the host institution and the funding agency, you must do four things:

1  Produce an accurate and comprehensive list of projected costs for your grant application.
2  Price your project in a way that suits both host institution and funding agency.
3  Show that your project offers value for money.
4  Use the costing methodology dictated by the funding agency (e.g. 'full economic costing' for a range of UK funding agencies).

These are four rather different challenges and you will certainly need the help of specialist finance colleagues with the second and fourth items on the list. You may also find that meeting one of the challenges appears to create conflicts with another. The rest of this chapter helps you meet each challenge without compromising the other three.

### Cost

Your first and obvious challenge is to cost all the resources you need to run your project. This means deciding how much of each item, resource or service you need and how much you need to pay for each of them.

This can be hard with a research project that only exists on paper and that may need changes of plan along the way. Some items on your list may also be very difficult to cost properly. However, you must produce an itemised budget that is comprehensive and specific for the project you describe in the application.

This budget must appear realistic, adequate and accurate to the decision makers. As referees and committee members have little knowledge of your research area, your application will need to provide evidence that your project budget meets these three criteria.

## Price

The price of your project is usually the sum of all the costs plus any overhead. However, the eventual price you put on your project may vary from the original cost if:

- There are tactical reasons for pricing your project at a particular level (e.g. funding agency expectations). Consequently, you may need to amend your project design in order to control your costs.
- The overhead is variable or optional. In this case, decide whether the maximum overhead is likely to be acceptable to the funding agency for this particular project.
- The funding agency has no set formula for the pricing of investigator time. Again, you must decide how high you can go while remaining competitive against other bidders.

At this point you may experience a difference of opinion with your employer as prospective host institution. Your priority may be to cover your direct research expenses. Meanwhile, your employer may expect your budget to contribute towards fixed and indirect costs, such as central services, space used, your salary and administrative support. They may even add specific items such as external audit fees if regular project audits are required by the funding agency.

## Value

Pricing issues should be resolved by considering the value of the project. Ultimately, you need to propose a project that referees and committee members consider value for money. Otherwise it will not win funding, no matter how well you have calibrated its cost and price.

A project that offers value for money has the following qualities:

- The importance of answering the research question justifies the expense in doing so
- The funding agency's investment has a high chance of a return through successful completion of the project and its outputs

In order to make this judgement, you can take two routes:

- Ask experienced referees, committee members and award holders for their opinion
- Look at previously-funded projects from the same funding agency and pay special attention to those that deal with similar questions or that cover the same field

In research funding competitions, value for money judgements are made in comparison with other applications. Consequently, checking what the funding agency typically invests in projects of your type will give you some useful points of comparison.

## Method

Some funding agencies (especially national government-sponsored organisations) have set formulas for calculating and presenting research grant budgets. You need the help of finance or research administration colleagues in order to produce a budget that is accurate and acceptable.

Some, like the UK's 'full economic costing', still elude the comprehension of experienced researchers years after their introduction. In the worst case scenario, applicants assume that a research grant will not cover the costs of any project they propose and hold back from applying. At the other end of the scale, researchers develop time-consuming proposals only to discover that their project will need financial top-ups from another source.

There are two simple rules to follow in order to avoid either trap:

- Check the feasibility of your project with a finance or administrative colleague with first-hand experience of the relevant costing methodology
- Do not be put off by well-meaning advice from colleagues who think they understand the methodology but do not

# Calculating your budget

Before addressing the price or value of your project, your first task is to work out what resources you need, how much of each resource you need and how much each resource should cost.

## Project staff

On research grants of any size, staff time is generally the major expense. This cost is usually calculated by Research or Finance Office colleagues on your behalf.

## Predicting staffing requirements

As you design your project, you need to consider who will carry out each of the required tasks, what skills the staff member will need to carry out each task and how much time it will take.

Unless you are applying for a fellowship, your project will usually involve two or more of the following:

- Principal Investigator
- Co-Investigator
- Post-doctoral research associate (PDRA)
- Research assistant (RA)
- Casual/hourly paid research assistant
- Project student
- Technician
- Administrative and clerical support
- Consultants

Some of these team members will be existing employees spending some of their time on the project and some will be hired as project staff. Funding agency rules dictate whether all these categories of staff are eligible costs. The maximum award limit and your own judgement will dictate the staffing levels you request.

As a major project expense, staffing levels come under close scrutiny by funding agency referees and committee members. If they decide that your project staff levels are insufficient, excessive or inappropriate, then you face rejection. Consequently, try to calculate staff costs accurately and justify your decisions throughout your case for support.

In order to choose the best way to staff your project, use the following two criteria:

- Are my proposed staffing levels sufficient to carry out all the components of the project?
- What are the norms for funded projects in my field and with this funding agency? It is probably easier to design a project that approximates to these norms than to convince a funding agency to approve a highly eccentric staffing pattern.

If you are a first-time applicant, calculating staff costs is laborious, especially if you try to do so in isolation. As mentioned in the previous section, asking advice and checking how similar funded projects were staffed will provide useful guidance.

## Calculating staff costs

Staff costs are the principal component of most project grant budgets. In order to obtain the correct figures from your Research or Finance Office, you will need to supply the following information about each prospective team member:

- Funding agency and scheme
- Start and end date of project
- Start and end date of employment on project
- Full or part time (and what percentage part time)
- Grading or level of duties to be undertaken
- Any information that makes the position non-standard (see below)

Using the official salary scales, they give you the correct price for that funding agency. This includes some combination of basic salary, social security, pension contributions, inflation, and future pay awards depending on individual agency rules. Administrative colleagues may need several working days in order to produce your staff costs and will have to recalculate the figure if you change any of the parameters.

Once you have established the cost of project staff, you can predict the overall cost of the project and finalise the design.

Watch out for the following:

- If you change any of the parameters (such as start date or funding agency) the staff costs will change. This is why you can rarely cut and paste costs from one grant application to another even if the staff requirements are very similar.
- Funding agency rules determine whether you can add clerical or technical support as additional items. Some funding agencies expect the host institution to supply these services in return for the overhead payment.
- Employment and tax law can play an important role in shaping your budget and, ultimately, the design of your project. This may apply to non-standard research staff such as overseas field workers or freelance consultants. This may mean that you need to hire project staff in a way that does not automatically suit you, your prospective employee or the project itself. Never assume that unusual or informal employment patterns are acceptable to either the host institution or funding agency.

## Investigator time and teaching replacement

Certain funding agencies reimburse the host institution for the time that researchers spend working on a funded project. The applicant nominates the number of hours that existing employees will each devote to the project and this is added to the total budget.

As with project staff, there are regulations, official guidance and accepted conventions that cover how much time you should devote to the funded project. Whatever level of investigator time you choose to include, you must provide a careful justification for the hours specified.

One way of estimating your time on the project is to calculate how many hours each task might take. For example, you might allow two hours per week for postgraduate supervision, one hour per week for staff supervision and 50 hours for organising a dissemination event. This process will prove very useful when you come to justify your budget.

Most academic employers outside the USA pay a 12-month salary irrespective of research grant success. This means that investigator time effectively forms part of the project overhead and is not classed as a direct expense of the project. Consequently, the host institution can choose how to allocate salary recovery unless the funding agency states how they are to be used.

However, the Principal Investigator may be able to negotiate with the host institution for relief from teaching and administration duties on this basis. In order to maintain a strong position in this negotiation, hold your discussion before the application is submitted and the grant is awarded.

Watch out for the following:

- If your teaching is in a highly specialist area with no obvious candidate to replace you, it will be important to negotiate hard and early on in the process. Do not wait until the grant is awarded as you will not have much room for manoeuvre. It is best to make any demands and get your head of department to agree to them in writing before you submit your application. This is especially important in the case of existing staff time, where the funding agency does not specify that the grant should be used to relieve the investigating team of other duties.
- Investigator time is calculated as a fraction of your actual salary. If you are a highly paid professor, this makes your projects more expensive. This may not affect any value for money arguments but could restrict other project expenses if the funding agency has a maximum award value.
- Some countries expect researchers to use grant income to supplement their own salary and this can prove problematic for international collaborations. If the funding agency does not accommodate this convention or make exceptions, researchers on restricted salaries may find it hard to participate.

## Project students

The funding agency will usually specify a stipend and how fees should be dealt with within the project budget. If the funding agency is based in your home country, it is likely to follow local conventions on this matter.

Watch out for the following:

- The issue of project studentships can become more complicated when the funding agency is based in a different country and may have different conventions and standards. Any substantial variation from home country practice may cause considerable legal and administrative complications for the host institution.

- Funding agencies often expect special justification for project students. This is to ensure that their inclusion is for the good of the project and the prospective student. Referees and committee members will be on the lookout for any ulterior motives, such as cheap labour or boosting postgraduate student numbers.

## Travel

Travel is another common component of research grants and you must itemise and justify each trip. Including an 'allowance' for general travel or conference attendance is not usually acceptable. Needless to say, you must also demonstrate that each journey is essential to the conduct or dissemination of the project.

Both the funding agency and your host institution may have set rates and guidance for travel, subsistence, accommodation and mileage. In any case, you should base each trip on the average economy fare to a destination and include any other necessary costs.

Depending of the type of trip, these might include airport transfers, visas, conference registration fees, local travel, car hire and short-term accommodation rental for longer trips.

Your budget must cover the actual cost of each journey and each trip needs specific justification. The timing, duration and frequency of project travel comes under as much scrutiny as the overall cost when your application is assessed.

Watch out for the following:

- Projects featuring extensive travel to attractive destinations tend to receive hostile scrutiny from referees and grants' committee members.
- If you have Co-Investigators, post-doctoral research associates and project students involved in your project, it may raise a few eyebrows if all the desirable project travel is earmarked for the Principal Investigator.
- Include a mix of travel and Skype or video conferencing for regular collaborator meetings.
- If you want to keep your overall budget down, do not quote unrealistically low travel costs in your application. It makes your project look poorly planned and may raise questions about its feasibility.
- Longer-term visits will appear more economical if you find self-catering accommodation on a short-term rental basis rather than hotels and full subsistence.

## Events

Workshops, symposia, exhibitions, conferences and steering groups are features of many research grant applications. Formal events and meetings are a useful way of structuring a project. They also help demonstrate that it will be well managed and that outcomes will be fully disseminated.

However, working out how much each event might cost can be a real challenge for academics with limited event management experience.

If left to your own devices on this matter, you must consider the following:

1  What types of event do you want to include?
2  How many of each of them will take place?
3  Where will they take place (location and venue)?
4  How long will each last?
5  How many people will participate in each event?

Until you answer these questions, you cannot start calculating your events budget. If you are clear on these points, then you can identify likely costs, as follows:

1  Will you need to pay for the travel, subsistence or accommodation for the participants? How many of them? Where will paid attendees be travelling from and will they need to stay overnight?
2  Will any attendees or other organisations contribute to the cost either financially or in kind (e.g. free venue hire or room booking)? Will the event generate any income?
3  Do you need to provide any catering or refreshments? If so, how many meals do you need to provide for how many people? Which meals? How often do you need to provide tea, coffee or water and for how many people?
4  In addition to hiring a venue, do you need to pay for audio-visual equipment, conference packs, signage, badges or posters?
5  Who will organise the event and/or help out on the day? Do you need to pay them to do so from the research grant?

Answering each of these questions will help clarify the costs. Add each new cost to a spreadsheet so that you can vary the parameters or multiply the number of events in order to reach your final figure.

## Equipment and facilities

Your funding agency will provide guidance on procedures for adding equipment costs to your research grant application. The host institution may also have its own purchasing and financial procedures that you need to follow. In any case, obtain a number of written quotations and follow instructions as regards additional items like software or maintenance contracts.

While your Research or Finance Office may not take responsibility for obtaining equipment costs on your behalf, you should discuss your plans with them and give them the opportunity to resolve any issues before the deadline.

Watch out for the following:

- You will usually need to include sales tax or import duty (where applicable) in the final budget. This will increase the overall costs and may have implications if you want to keep the total budget below a certain level.
- If you are importing an item, the host institution usually specifies the exchange rate. This is likely to be cautious and may appear to inflate the cost of the equipment.
- Expensive equipment can sometimes unbalance a grant application budget if overhead rates are low or linked to staff costs. This may be exacerbated if your institution top slices research income.

## Services and consultancy

There may be tasks associated with your proposed project that no member of the project team has the skills or time to carry out. Examples might include creating a website, running a large-scale survey, and transcribing or translating documents. Each of these items is a fixed cost and may cause some of the same issues as equipment.

Watch out for the following:

- If you 'employ' staff on a research grant through fixed consultancy payments, these costs are not eligible for overhead payments linked to project staff or investigators.
- Paying individuals as consultants has legal implications regarding where and how they can work for your project.
- Consultants are not covered by your employer's liability insurance and will need to organise their own policy.
- In addition, they do not benefit from holiday, sick pay or pension contributions and this lack of security usually means much higher hourly rates.

## Justifying your budget

Your research grant application must tell the funding agency why each budget item is essential to your project. It is not enough to show that your budget is accurate and sufficient. You must also explain why you need each resource and how they will all be used to carry out the proposed programme.

The funding agency may provide a section of the application form in which you justify your budget. However you must also show that your budget is necessary, sufficient and offers good value for money throughout the application.

By the time referees and committee members read as far as the full budget and justification section, there should be no surprises. The case for support is, in particular, critical to convincing the funding agency that your project is worth the sum you request.

In a typical, full-length application format you should take the following opportunities to describe or justify resources and support the *value* proposition.

| | |
|---|---|
| Abstract/Summary | Mention the duration and principal costs, e.g. 'During this three year project, two postdoctoral research associates will run ten experiments under the direction of the Principal Investigator while the project student and Co-Investigator will...'. |
| Plan of investigation | Mention of each relevant resource and how it will be used at each stage of the proposed programme is described in depth, e.g. 'Five three-day visits to the archive in Ghent will give the Research Associate and Co-Investigator the opportunity to...'. |
| Budget | Itemise each resource and give as much detail as possible against each cost given, e.g. '1 × 5-day trip to the International Scientific Conference in China for the Principal Investigator and project student, incl. flights, transfers, accommodation, subsistence, visas and registration fees'. |
| Justification | Summarise why you need each resource in turn, e.g. 'In order to organise, conduct and analyse 50 hour-long interviews, we anticipate that we will need a full-time postdoctoral research associate for 9 months'. |

In summary, ensure that each item included in the budget is also mentioned at least once in the case for support. This helps referees and committee members understand how each cost fits in with the project.

══════════════ **TOOL 15** ══════════════

## IS IT WORTH IT?

Start by making a rough list of the resources essential to conducting research in your field. These might include the following:

- Project staff (how many, for how long, at what level of seniority)
- Investigator time or teaching replacement (especially if teaching or admin relief is essential to the conduct of the project)
- Project studentships
- Collaborator input (especially if overseas)
- PCs or laptops for research team
- Equipment
- Access to (scientific) facilities
- (Scientific) consumables
- Travel, accommodation and subsistence

- Large sub-contracted items (e.g. surveys)
- Specialist services or consultancy (e.g. web design)
- Publication costs

Funding agencies publish a lists of eligible and ineligible costs as well as maximum award values. Check your resources list off against this information and consider the impact any ineligible items will have on your proposed projects.

---

## TOOL 16

# INTELLIGENT QUESTIONS ABOUT FINANCE

This Tool helps you consider how well a particular funding agency or scheme works for your project and host institution. Once you have a plan for your budget, ask your Research or Finance Office the following questions:

### Do my proposed costs fit between the lower and upper limit of the funding scheme?

This is important as a generous-sounding upper limit may include substantial overheads that restrict your direct project expenses.

### Are there any elements of my required resources that are likely to cause a funding shortfall with this particular scheme?

Certain funding agencies only provide a percentage of direct research expenses. Consequently, the host institution has to ensure that overheads, an institutional commitment or some form of match funding are sufficient to cover the full cost of the project. This means that your budget may need to be carefully constructed in order to ensure a particular balance between specific categories of cost items.

### Does the scheme offer overheads? If yes...

### Does this mean that this project, if awarded, will generate a surplus?

A research grant with overheads generally brings your institution more money than the direct research expenses of the project. This will make the grant especially attractive to your employer.

### How big will this surplus be for this particular project?

Your Research or Finance Office should be able to calculate how much surplus a particular research grant application will generate.

---

### Is any of the surplus allocated to my personal research account?

As your employer hosts the project, you have no automatic access to any overhead attached to the grant. If you have ideas about how this money should be spent, you must negotiate before your submit the application.

### Which project costs is the overhead expected to cover?

If a funding agency offers overheads, there will usually be guidance on the purpose of the overhead. Generally, overheads (or indirect costs) are an acknowledgement of the expense of hosting a project and include items such as office space, administrative support and shared central resources. The funding agency may offer broad guidance as to how overheads should be used but leave the final decision to the host institution.

### Does this mean I cannot add project consumables, technical support, or office supplies to my budget?

As above, an overhead payment may come with a list of ineligible items that any overhead or indirect costs should cover. Make sure that your employer understands this requirement.

### If I win a grant that funds investigator time, do I automatically get relief from teaching or administrative duties?

If you want relief from other duties, you need to negotiate this before you submit the grant application. This process should allow you and your employer to decide whether your project is financially viable and ensure that you do not proceed with false assumptions about how the grant, if awarded, will be allocated internally.

## Conclusion

After reading this chapter, you should be able to calculate the right budget for every research grant application. This includes both calculating accurate budgets and ensuring that all your project costs are eligible. You should also be aware of the possible pitfalls and issues that you need to resolve before submitting your applications.

# THIRTEEN

## HOW TO PUT TOGETHER COLLABORATIVE PROJECTS

This chapter addresses the challenge of writing collaborative research grant applications. It suggests a number of techniques that help convince decision makers to support complex projects and discusses ways in which large collaborative applications differ from single applicant bids.

There are three Tools within this chapter. *The Collaboration Checklist* helps you decide whether to invest time and energy into a particular consortium. Meanwhile, the *Collaborative Project Agenda* addresses the preparatory and behind-the-scenes issues that can prevent workable collaborations. Finally, *Produce Your Evidence II (Collaboration)* considers the different approach needed to create a fundable collaborative application.

## Introduction

The basic principles of successful grant-writing generally apply to collaborative research grant applications. However, there are some additional challenges you must meet when seeking research funding for large-scale projects with multiple partners. There are also some instances when you may need to adapt your approach to meet the needs of complex and highly-specified funding schemes.

Although there are many schemes that support small collaborations and short-term partnerships, making fundable application to schemes of this sort is reasonably straightforward. However, convincing decision makers to fund a long, expensive multi-site or multi-disciplinary project presents particular challenges.

The longer and more complex a project, the more opportunity it has to fail. At application stage, effectively supporting the *success* proposition is crucial. This chapter concentrates on these complex, large-scale applications.

Your first task is to understand both the advantages and drawbacks of engaging with this type of funded research. Involvement in large collaborative applications and projects involves higher levels of effort and lower success rates. Unless you weigh these up carefully you may waste large amounts of your time on no-hope applications.

Once you have decided to go ahead, you must consider the following if you are to create a fundable collaborative bid:

- An understanding of the funding agency's motives in offering collaborative grants. Each agency has its own agenda, which is determined by political, charitable, scientific or commercial factors. If your project does not support the overall aim of the scheme (however well it tackles the research question), you will not be successful.
- A balance between agency requirements regarding the scale of your consortium and what resources you actually need to answer the research question successfully. This means designing a workable and cost-effective project within quite strict political or bureaucratic constraints.

In addition, collaborative research grant applications present a number of grant-writing challenges. In brief, your application document must do some or all of the following:

- Make a long-term multi-site or multi-disciplinary project easy to understand and easy to remember
- Convince decision makers that a project created within 'artificial' parameters is exciting and achievable
- Defend each aspect of your project effectively from the larger number of non-specialist decision makers tasked to evaluate larger projects

As a consequence, acting as Principal Investigator on a research grant application of this scale is very difficult without previous experience in winning large grants.

Applicants to funding agencies with idiosyncratic requirements, such as the European Commission, often take advantage of professional training or bid-writing services in order to improve their likelihood of success. Your chances as an inexperienced applicant who tries to work in isolation are slim.

Even for less complex schemes, expect to compete against established consortia with experience in the area and insider knowledge of the funding agency. Trying to build a consortium from scratch with a minimal track record is not a competitive starting point for a large collaborative bid.

The rest of this chapter discusses each of the key challenges to successful collaborative grant-writing. It also considers what to do when a large collaborative project is rejected by a funding agency.

# Why collaborate?

Success in high-profile collaborative schemes is career enhancing and academic employers encourage collaboration. However, there may be other factors that attract you to large collaborative project:

- Your research questions can only be answered through a multi-site or multi-disciplinary approach
- You want to facilitate existing partnerships outside your institution with external funding
- You are invited to join a consortium and the opportunity appears to require minimal effort or a high chance of success

None of these reasons is inherently problematic. However, there are a series of considerations that may make you think twice about some collaborative funding opportunities:

- Many dedicated collaborative funding schemes – such as European Commission calls or UK Research Council managed programmes – have very low success rates.
- Funding agency guidance alone may not be enough to help you prepare a successful application to one of these high-profile collaborative schemes. Further advice may be necessary in order to understand the type of consortium or project that is most likely to be successful. You may also need help in decoding the guidance and understanding how it translates into successful proposals.
- Coordinating a collaborative bid as lead applicant is extremely time consuming and requires strong management skills. Equally, playing a small part in a larger consortium may leave you in a 'journeyman' role where you provide specific technical skills but get no publishable output.
- Projects inspired by cross-disciplinary calls for proposals do not always lead to high-profile publications in leading journals.
- Multi-disciplinary applications must appeal to decision makers who have no expertise in some of the participating disciplines. This can reduce their chance of success, especially when they are in competition with single discipline bids.

This means that collaborative funding opportunities always need careful consideration. Avoid getting involved in no-hope consortia or becoming entangled in poorly-managed, poorly-resourced projects that damage you professionally.

The following Tool will help you decide whether to commit to a large-scale collaborative application.

================================ TOOL 17 ================================

## THE COLLABORATION CHECKLIST

Before agreeing to join a consortium, ask the following questions:

- What sort of discipline and/or institution leads successful applications to this scheme? What is the success rate of the scheme? You can find this information from the funding agency.
- Does the Principal Investigator have the track record to lead a project of this scale and complexity (see Chapter 1)? Has he or she managed at least one three-year project grant with a team of postdoctoral researchers? If not, the funding agency may be reluctant to award a large grant to an untried research team.
- Is the proposed role and contribution of each partner clear at an early stage in the application process? A lack of organisation is usually apparent in the application document itself and affects your chance of success.
- What will the project bring to you in terms of:
  - Grant income or access to resources? Check the eligible costs of the scheme with the funding agency and find out what share will come to your institution. There is no point committing to a project that takes up a large proportion of your time but only provides enough money to cover a few travel expenses.
  - Networking opportunities? Who else is involved? Are these researchers with whom you would like to develop closer working relationships? If so, working together on the application may bring future benefits whether the project is funded or not.
  - Access to publishable outputs? Will the research project itself lead to worthwhile publications for you? Unless the project generates a disproportionate amount of research income, funded research that does not lead to publication is of questionable value.
  - Project management experience? What will your role be within the project? What elements will you manage? If involvement in the funded project will enhance your CV as a future project leader, then you should consider accepting the invitation.
- How much time will you need to invest in preparing the application? Weigh this up against the success rate of the scheme and the track record of the Principal Investigator before you commit.
- How does the Principal Investigator propose that the consortium works together in order to prepare a fundable application (e.g. meetings, Skype, agreed timetable leading up to the deadline)?
- Will the resources available through the scheme allow you to carry out your part of the project effectively?

- Does your employer consider the scheme financially viable? (See Chapters 6 and 12 for more information). Some schemes have elaborate requirements for institutional match funding or very restricted eligible costs that make them unattractive to particular host institutions.

In the light of these answers, do you consider that this collaboration:

- Has a reasonable chance of success?
- Is likely to be well managed by the Principal Investigator?
- Will bring you sufficient benefit in terms of income, publications and building your personal research network?
- Is likely to answer the research question successfully?

If so, it is worth getting involved. If not, you will be better off targeting more realistic research funding opportunities.

# Why fund collaborations?

Funding agencies have specific reasons for setting up schemes that aim to support collaborative research. These include the following:

- Cooperation between different countries or regions
- Enhancing research capacity in certain areas or categories of organisation (e.g. developing countries, businesses, public sector organisations)
- Generating innovative answers to research problems or themes by encouraging different disciplines to work together
- Promoting partnerships between established research institutions and organisations in geographical areas or sectors that have a less developed research infrastructure

In order to gauge whether your project has a chance of success in a collaborative funding competition, you need to understand the funding agency's agenda. Even if your proposed consortium seems appropriate in terms of its scale and membership, there is no point in proceeding if your project does not also meet the objectives of the scheme.

EXAMPLE 36

## WHY AGENCIES FUND COLLABORATIONS

Here are a few examples of the reasons funding agencies give for supporting collaborative research:

**EC The Seventh Framework Programme (FP7): Cooperation[30]**

The specific programme on '**Cooperation**' supports all types of research activities carried out by different research bodies in trans-national cooperation and aims to gain or consolidate leadership in key scientific and technology areas.

**Leverhulme Trust: Programme Grants[31]**

The scale of the awards ... is set at a level where it is possible for a research team to study a significant theme in depth by conducting a group of interlinked research projects which, taken together, can lead to new understanding. The themes are selected not to exclude particular disciplines from the competition but rather to encourage research teams to look upon their established research interests from a set of refreshing viewpoints.

**Research Councils UK: Cross Council Research Themes[32]**

Novel, multidisciplinary approaches are needed to solve many, if not all, of the big research challenges over the next 10 to 20 years. To achieve this, RCUK will coordinate the delivery of multidisciplinary research in seven priority areas. Each theme is important in terms of the knowledge and skilled people which will be generated, and has significant potential for delivering economic impact.

For more detail on how to find this sort of information about your target funding agencies, please refer to Appendix 2.

Once you identify the aim of the scheme, make the fit between your project and the scheme explicit. Demonstrating how your project serves the agency's agenda is a key part of establishing the importance of your project in a managed collaborative competition.

Use Tool 13 in Chapter 9 to produce evidence on how your project serves the agency agenda and include it prominently in strategic parts of your application document.

# Workable collaborations

A collaborative grant application that results in a workable project needs a lot of behind-the-scenes discussion and negotiation that may not be apparent in the application document itself.

---

[30]http://cordis.europa.eu/fp7/cooperation/home_en.html (last accessed 20 October 2011)
[31]www.leverhulme.ac.uk/funding/RP/RP.cfm (last accessed 20 October 2011)
[32]www.rcuk.ac.uk/research/xrcprogrammes/Pages/home.aspx (last accessed 20 October 2011)

There is a paradox here. On one hand, the funding agency holds all the cards as projects that do not meet the agency criteria have no chance whatsoever. On the other, a collaborative project may look very promising on paper but prove unworkable, thanks to personality clashes or an unprofessional attitude within the consortium. Whatever the benefits of research grant success, there is no point in winning a large grant if the project is doomed to failure.

The tension between 'fundable' and 'workable' projects arises whatever your starting point, and might include any of the following:

1  **Call for proposals**. The applicants design a project that responds to a specific research question or theme and/or with a consortium that also meets the agency's requirements. Their challenge is to show that they will articulate and answer the question more successfully than competing consortia. However, if they feel that the agency criteria work against the most efficient or effective solution to the research problem, they are not at liberty to change the parameters. They also risk creating a consortium that looks attractive to the funding agency but does not prove workable in practice.

2  **Existing research collaboration**. The applicants target a scheme with a project idea developed within an existing partnership. These applicants must convince decision makers that their question is worth answering and that the proposed partnership is the best way of doing so. If the consortium includes superfluous partners who cannot be excluded for political or social reasons, then fundability of the bid is compromised. It may also be difficult to find a funding scheme that meets the needs of every partner who would like to be involved in the application.

3  **Research question**. Applicants create a partnership to answer a specific research question and then search for a suitable scheme. In many ways, this is the most logical and straightforward approach to funding collaborative research, although it relies on finding a scheme that fits both the question and the proposed partnership. This is not always possible.

In order to avoid the problems inherent in each of these three scenarios, you must take the following steps:

First, only commit to partners you trust and will enjoy working with. Otherwise the project, if funded, will offer nothing but misery from start to finish. In the case of large collaborative funding schemes (such as those offered by the European Commission), you are unlikely to put together a workable consortium from scratch and produce a fundable application in the time between the publication of the Call for Proposals and the deadline. Consequently, pre-existing partnerships have an advantage over artificially-constructed consortia and the best collaborations develop naturally.

Secondly, test the 'workability' of your project without considering agency criteria. Does the project appear logically and appropriately resourced? Do any of the partners appear superfluous? Are any important resources missing?

Thirdly, find effective ways of communicating with your partners, negotiating the terms of your potential collaboration and ensuring mutual understanding. This process has two elements:

- If you are working with collaborators from different disciplines, sectors or countries, you may experience communication difficulties. Cultural and linguistic differences, technical terminology and professional expectations may cause problems if all key issues and terminology are not clarified at an early stage.
- The collaboration must be properly and formally constituted before you submit the application. Issues such as project and financial management, reporting, division of resources and intellectual property must be agreed and set out in writing in advance.

This behind-the-scenes work may not be explicit in the application document itself but is essential if a funded collaboration is to succeed. The following Tool is designed to help you produce a workable collaboration.

========================= TOOL 18 =========================

## THE COLLABORATIVE PROJECT AGENDA

Throughout your project negotiation, you need to meet (in person or virtually) with all partners and agree the following points before the application is finalised and submitted. The points on the agenda for this 'meeting' should include:

- Resources that each member of the consortium will provide (access to participants, equipment, office space, etc.)
- Resources that each member of the consortium needs in order to conduct their element of the project
- Any discrepancy between resources needed and the eligible costs of the funding agency
- The ownership of intellectual property rights and/or authorship of papers
- How the project will be formally managed and governed
  - Reporting lines
  - Financial management
  - Line management of staff
  - Supervision of students
  - Producing funding agency reports
- How progress will be assessed and decisions taken

In consultation with colleagues from your Research, Finance or Enterprise Offices, you then need to make sure that your decisions are properly documented and formally agreed. Some of this information will be included in the grant application document itself and other elements will be the subject of memoranda of understanding or partnership agreements that are legally-binding to the signatories.

Only when you have established that your proposed consortium is workable should you commit yourself to the grant application.

---

# Convincing collaborations

Assembling a workable consortium that also meets the requirements of the funding scheme is the first challenge to putting together a fundable application. The second challenge is to describe the proposed collaboration convincingly.

Inevitably, there is overlap between the two challenges, but there is a difference between a potentially effective collaboration and one that is described convincingly. First, it is possible to leave out information about the potentially effective collaboration that makes it impossible for decision makers to support the application. Secondly, very complex and specific evaluation criteria may not favour the most effective collaborations.

This is where previous experience and insider knowledge come in particularly useful. In order to succeed with this type of scheme, you may need help in reading between the lines of agency guidance and understanding what factors ensure a positive evaluation.

That aside, a collaborative research grant application has the same function as any other grant application. In brief, it must make your project seem more important than other applications in the same competition. Given this, you must keep in mind the parameters of your target funding scheme and what the key points of comparison are likely to be.

Inevitably, this depends on the individual funding scheme. How you convince decision makers to support your particular project depends on the nature of competing applications:

1   **They address the same research questions set by the funding scheme**. In this case, you do not need to justify the question itself. The emphasis must be on your ability to answer the question successfully. The decision makers will focus on your track record, your methods and the value for money of your approach.
2   **Every application takes an interdisciplinary approach to a project on the same theme**. In this case, you need to produce a striking research question and a consortium that provides an interesting response to the set topic.
3   **The scheme specifies consortia of similar size and composition**. In this case, you still need to show that your proposed consortium is the best way of answering the question. It is very important that you do not assume that any consortium that falls within the specified

---

range is fundable. The precise role and scientific contribution of each partner must always be clearly specified.

4   **Most of the other projects are single applicant or single discipline**. In this case, you have to provide strong justification for each element of your project. You will be in competition against more straightforward, easily-defensible projects. They may also be cheaper because they are based at one site or easier to understand because they include one discipline.

In order to produce the evidence that will convince decision makers to support your collaboration, you need to write with the following information in mind:

- The overall aim of the particular funding scheme
- The parameters of the competition
- The published evaluation criteria

Use the Tool at the end of this section to generate evidence supporting the four key propositions as they relate to large collaborative projects.

## Well-defended collaborations

In the context of a funding scheme with a set research topic and strict parameters on the composition of eligible consortia, producing a well-defended application is as important as creating an exciting project. In addition, a large collaborative project represents a large investment on the part of the funding agency. Consequently, there will be more caution in allocating the available funds.

In many cases, the funding agency has defined the question and provided a structure within which the question must be answered. Consequently, you need to justify and explain your choices within this framework.

This means paying special attention to:

- The specific role and active contribution of each partner
- Justifying each resource, including investigator hours and each member of staff
- The level of overheads requested (if this is variable)
- Deadlines and milestones for delivering various outputs
- Project management arrangements, including financial management and administration
- Project governance and ethical review, if necessary
- Compliance with funding agency reporting or audit requirements
- Dissemination programme

The resulting application document may not be the most exciting read in the world but it will prove hard to criticise and may fare better in the evaluation process than more flamboyant or seemingly innovative projects.

# Well-described collaborations

The application document for a long multi-site or multi-disciplinary application must include an enormous amount of information if decision makers are to understand the project sufficiently to support it. This must be achieved in a way that means referees and grants' committee members do not lose sight of the overall project aims and potential outcomes.

This information will include:

- A background section that takes literature from several disciplines into account
- A description of several sub-projects, including their individual research questions and methodological approaches
- A justification of a large set of resources spread across several sites
- A timetable of activity that includes a large team and several sites working together for up to five years
- An extensive programme of dissemination
- Project management, including team meetings and milestones

You must fit all of this within the limited word count of the funding agency template and keep the main points memorable.

In addition, defending a complex project against critical, non-specialist decision makers means that you must organise your arguments clearly and logically so that key information can be easily identified and accessed.

In Chapter 9, we introduced ways of presenting information effectively so that it stays within the working memory of non-specialist speed readers (see *Example 29: Chunking*). This looked at breaking up arguments into manageable chunks and using lists or bullet points in order to communicate clearly.

If you are writing a very complex collaborative grant application, this approach will not be sufficient. The best way of marshalling large quantities of information is through graphs, charts and tables. In the case of overall project management, a formal GANTT chart showing activity, milestones and deliverables may be mandatory.

The areas of your project that will certainly benefit from being presented this way include:

- Budget: expenditure by type, year, sub-project and site
- Activity: key milestones in the project, including planning, data collection, analysis and dissemination as well as meetings and deadlines for project deliverables
- Team: who is assigned to the project or employed to work on it, for what period, in what capacity and with what responsibility
- Institutions: what each partner institution provides or facilitates

Finally, there is one aspect of describing a complex collaborative project that requires a rather different approach from the standard, single applicant proposal. This is in the use of jargon. Particular schemes use esoteric jargon in describing their requirements and you are well advised to mimic this in your application document.

This does not give you a free rein to also use within-discipline jargon, but if the funding agency asks you to provide a 'chronograph', you should stick to the same vocabulary, however tortuous.

# Collaborative application development

In order to produce collaborative applications that are convincing, well-defended and well-described, you must take a different approach to constructing your application document.

Earlier in this book, we introduced the concept of four key propositions that each funding application must make in order to convince decision makers to support it. Tool 13 helped you produce the appropriate evidence and this chapter extends this tool to cover the additional demands of a large collaborative project.

---

**TOOL 19**

## PRODUCE YOUR EVIDENCE II (COLLABORATION)

This Tool looks the sorts of evidence you must produce in order to convince decision makers to support large collaborative projects.

### Proposition 1: This proposal asks an important question

When the funding agency sets the theme for a project, you must establish the importance of the question in a slightly different way. The agency already considers the question an important one and your task is to demonstrate that your response to the challenge set by the agency is not artificially induced. This leaves you with two tasks:

- To show that you also think the question is important by your previous work in this area
- To articulate a question that fits the criteria of the Call for Proposals and demonstrates its relative importance to the overall theme

---

THE RESEARCH FUNDING TOOLKIT

## Proposition 2: The project is likely to answer the question

In the case of large collaborative projects, project management is as important as methodology in demonstrating that you are likely to answer the question successfully. This is where the use of project management tools such as GANTT charts will be particularly important.

In particular, you need to provide evidence that shows how:

- Formal project management will mitigate risks, maximise outputs and aid completion
- You will complete a long, complex project in the time specified and with the resources specified
- Everyone involved in the project has a clear role

In addition, if your project is likely to be the only multi-disciplinary or multi-site project in the competition, you need to write defensively about your choice of an interdisciplinary or collaborative approach.

## Proposition 3: The likely gain from the project is worth the resources requested

As your project will be expensive, you need to show a range of high-impact outputs appropriate to the question.

Also consider the funding agency's overall objective in supporting collaborative research programmes. If one of the aims is to support international cooperation or build research capacity, show explicitly how this project achieves this.

You also need to demonstrate that all requested resources are necessary to the completion of the project. Where the funding agency specifies the scale and composition of eligible consortia, your application document must show that your consortium is appropriate to the project.

If the decision makers suspect that you have bolted on partners or activities to create an eligible project, they will not fund you. Consequently, you need to show that each partner has a role relevant to answering the research question.

Where a project involves a large team, show who is involved in each dissemination activity and in what capacity. Ensure that your dissemination plan is well articulated and covers all the relevant academic and user groups. In addition, there may be forms of dissemination currently favoured by the funding agency decision makers. You may be able to consult with agency insiders or consistently successful applicants in order to ascertain this.

**Proposition 4: The applicant and team are competent to carry out the project as described**

The Principal Investigator must have a substantial track record of bringing large, funded projects to a successful conclusion.

In addition, each member of the team must have the skills and experience necessary for the conduct of each element of the project. As well as the bundle of CVs that accompany your application, you should mention the relevant experience of each project partner in the text of your application document.

**Additional proposition 5: The institution is likely to support the research team appropriately**

When a project is designed to run over several institutions and in several countries the role of each institution will vary, but should nonetheless be defined. The lead institution may provide centralised project and financial management via dedicated administrators, while some partner institutions may only provide specialist technical or scientific input to one Work Programme.

In addition, it may be that some institutions benefit from the expertise or research infrastructure of other members of the consortium. Indeed, this may be a requirement of the scheme if one of the objectives is to develop research infrastructure. In this case, this activity will help meet the overall objective of the scheme and should be presented as a positive outcome.

---

# Rejection and resubmission

It is an unwelcome fact that large, complex collaborative grant applications take a long time to prepare and have a small chance of success. The specific demands of the funding agency regarding the scale and composition of consortia may also mean that your application is not immediately recyclable elsewhere.

It may be best to face up to this possibility at planning stage and commit to a collaborative grant application with this eventuality in mind. Consequently, one of your criteria for involvement may be looking at the benefits that involvement in the application might bring in terms of networking and generating further research ideas.

When faced with rejection you have the following options open to you:

- Using the existing collaboration to address a different question in a future Call for Proposals from the same funding scheme

- Submitting a related application to a different scheme with selected partners from the current collaboration (allowing for intellectual property rights, etc.)
- Taking your part of the project and submitting a single applicant proposal elsewhere

Whatever the outcome, make sure that your investment in a high-risk collaborative application has some intrinsic benefits.

# Conclusion

After reading this chapter, you should be aware of the particular demands made by large, collaborative research grant applications and be able to approach the application process accordingly. This involves organising large amounts of information and convincing a range of non-specialist decision makers to support a speculative investment in your research.

# APPENDIX 1
## HOW TO RUN 'TOOLKIT' WORKSHOPS

## Summary

This chapter shows how to put *The Research Funding Toolkit* techniques into practice across your institution. It is based on the principle that grant-writing requires a combination of skills and awareness. This means it is easier to develop the necessary skills and awareness within a supportive community of researchers than by working in isolation. This chapter proposes a programme of workshops and expert seminars that you can implement within your organisation to support this development process. Each of the workshop formats described in this chapter makes optimum use of your institution's senior researchers with grants' committee experience. The programme template also aims to give every potential applicant in your institution the chance to improve their grant-writing skills and those of their colleagues.

## Rationale

As discussed through the book, it is hard to develop a fundable research grant application without understanding the nature of research funding competitions.

In brief, these competitions are judged by groups of experienced researchers from a variety of fields who assess and rank applications using criteria set by the funding agency. It is a complex process and researchers have a greater chance of success if they understand:

- The competitive nature of the funding agency decision
- The needs, motivations and working conditions of referees and grants' committee members

- How to make their research projects exciting and important to a wider research community
- How to use funding agency application templates to communicate their research plans effectively

This book addresses all these issues but, as it points out consistently, applying the recommended techniques needs a wide perspective on your own research and specialist feedback.

Unfortunately, researchers tend to write grant applications in the same style as their books and journal articles. This does not account for the way that the two decision-making groups referees and grants' committee members read and use these documents. It also fails, to account for the knowledge levels and working conditions of the two decision-making groups.

In addition, applicants unknowingly attract misleading pre-submission feedback by approaching trusted colleagues within the same discipline. These close collaborators are doubly disqualified from providing useful feedback. First, they tend to take a within-discipline approach rather than applying the broad, non-specialist criteria used in most funding agency competitions. Secondly, they may be reluctant to seem critical of the applicant's project, especially if the deadline is only a couple of days away. As a consequence, they tend to provide unrealistically positive feedback on applications that have little chance of success in the competition.

This leaves researchers with unrealistic hopes about the likely success of their project. When their project is rejected, applicants feel misunderstood and angry with the funding agency. It does not occur to them that they asked the wrong people for the wrong sort of feedback. They may never learn that they need to take a new approach to application development.

This book explains how to design appropriate projects, write fundable applications and obtain appropriate feedback. However, researchers may need some help from their institution if they want to put these techniques into practice.

One problem your researchers may face is a lack of contact with colleagues who have insider experience of research funding competitions. Another is that they may have restricted access to appropriate feedback from other researchers. Finally, they may never have learned the specialist writing techniques that help their applications stand out against competitors.

The aim of this chapter is to describe a programme of expert workshops and seminars that provide solutions to these three problems. Fortunately, grant-writing skills are not discipline-specific and most grants' committees use similar scoring and ranking systems. Consequently, the fundamental principles of successful grant-writing are common to all disciplines.

This means that the advice of one grants' committee member is relevant to a wide range of researchers. Bringing applicants from diverse fields together in these workshops also helps provide the diversity of perspective that exists in real grants' committees.

This process means that applicants acquire the relevant knowledge and learn necessary skills from successful senior researchers and receive practical support from a wide community of colleagues as they work on individual project proposals.

# What applicants need to know

As discussed throughout this book, research grant applicants need a set of skills that are specific to the grant-writing process. There are six stages to winning research funding and applicants need specific skills and knowledge in order to succeed in each of them.

The proposed programme is modular and is based on the six stages of application development and an associated set of things that researchers 'need to know' in order to succeed at each stage. They are, as follows:

### Process Stage 1: Understand the competitive evaluation process used by funding agencies

For some researchers, understanding the grant-giving process is their stumbling block. Once they understand the following points, they can apply them to the way they design projects and write their applications:

- Research grant applications are assessed by a wide range of busy academics who are usually neither specialists in your field, nor enthusiasts for it
- Funding agencies make speculative investments and need to be confident in the likely success of the proposed project
- Grant applications are assessed in competition with other applications from different areas
- Success rates are low and funding agencies are forced to reject many applications for high-quality projects

### Process Stage 2: Ensure that your research questions and projects stand out against others in the same competition

For some researchers, developing projects that stand up to the competitive, multi-disciplinary environment of research grant competitions is the challenge. Consequently, they need to learn how to meet the first two 'key propositions' of fundable projects described earlier in this book:

- Design research questions that still seem important in the context of a research grant competition (i.e. the *importance* proposition)
- Design projects that are likely to answer the question (i.e. the *success* proposition)

## Process Stage 3: Understand that research grants are speculative investments and that your application must provide evidence that the funding agency's investment is likely to pay off

For some researchers, the challenge is to demonstrate that their project is a worthwhile investment and unlikely to waste the funding agency's money. This means they need to learn how to meet the rest of the 'key propositions' and provide the necessary evidence in their research grant applications:

- Design projects that are value for money and worth the resources requested (i.e. the *value* proposition)
- Design projects that the applicant and team can objectively show that they are competent to carry out (i.e. the *competence* proposition)
- Understand how to generate evidence that supports all four propositions and matches funding agency evaluation criteria

## Process Stage 4: Make your applications easy for researchers from outside your discipline to read and understand

The fourth stage of the process involves specialist grant-writing skills. Many well-designed projects fall down at this stage and applicants must learn how to:

- Make applications as exciting and convincing as possible for referees and grants' committee members
- Write applications that are easy for busy people to speed-read
- Write applications that are easy for a wide range of fellow researchers to understand

## Process Stage 5: Seek feedback to ensure that every application you submit has no weak points

In order to ensure a well-defended application, applicants must know how to:

- Obtain the right sort of feedback from the right sort of people
- Give appropriate feedback in return

## Process Stage 6: Find ways of dealing with low success rates by submitting high-quality applications as quickly and as frequently as possible

Some applicants submit fundable applications but not frequently enough to have a good chance of winning a grant. In order to understand how to streamline the process and improve their chances they need to:

- Understand the generic functions and structure of funding agency templates
- Understand how different parts of the typical template relate to each other and are used by referees and grants' committee members
- Understand how to produce a batch of different applications based on similar ideas and techniques

The rest of this chapter explains how to create an institutional programme of expert seminars and workshops that help researchers acquire the skills and knowledge needed to succeed in each of these six stages.

# Basic principles

However you organise your programme, it will only work if you stick to six basic principles. If you cannot do this, then a cross-institutional programme may not be appropriate:

1  **Leaders.** Every session must be led by senior academics with good communication skills and grants' committee experience. There is no point in wheeling out senior managers or directors of research if they do not have this. Their advice may be misleading. It may also be tempting to use successful applicants or regular referees for major funding agencies to lead sessions. You should also avoid doing this as their advice will not be informed by the all-important grants' committee experience. Equally, these sessions should not be delivered by administrators. Their advice may be accurate but they will lack credibility with academic participants and give sessions a 'corporate' flavour. If necessary, you may have to hire in this expertise.

2  **Content.** The content of the sessions should be developed in conjunction with the speaker or session leaders. If your leaders are successful researchers with extensive grants' committee experience and a strong track record of winning grants, they don't need to read this book first. They will have a clear understanding about what applicants must do to create fundable proposals. In addition, the titles of events and topics covered should appeal to the anxieties and concerns of the participants (not those of the organisers).

3  **Style.** The sessions must all be informal. Management speak and corporate training techniques should be avoided.

4  **Timing.** Every session must be easy for a busy academic to attend, i.e. short sessions, conveniently timed and in accessible locations. Workshops should run throughout the year, with an emphasis on periods when researchers are actively preparing grant applications. This allows participants to apply techniques as they develop applications.

5  **Attendance.** Attendance at events should not be forced or confined to certain groups – single discipline workshops are counterproductive. Providing refreshments is a very useful way to encourage maximum attendance.

6  **Support**. One-to-one administrative support on application developments (budgets, targeting funding agencies, bureaucracy, etc.) must be provided outside these sessions to avoid queries and discussions that are irrelevant to most participants.

# Resources

How you put together a programme for your institution will depend on a number of factors. The principal issue to consider is the research profile of your organisation. A leading university that needs constant research income to support equipment and laboratories has different needs from a less research-intensive institution where research grants are a rarity. The availability of grants' committee members, the number of potential participants and the general research culture will all affect your choices.

If you have answers to the following (or estimates), you have enough information to get started:

- The number of staff within the institution who are eligible or qualified to apply for external research grants, i.e.:
  - They hold permanent academic contracts
  - They hold PhDs or are of post-doctoral standing
  - They publish in peer reviewed journals, within edited collections, write research monographs or present papers at academic conferences

- The proportion of active researchers who:
  - Have ever applied for research grants
  - Have ever won research funding
  - Apply for grants regularly (at least one substantial application every year)
  - Win grants regularly (at least one success every two years)
  - Consider that winning research grants is important

- The number of senior researchers within the organisation who are qualified to lead sessions, i.e.:
  - They sit on grants' committees
  - They are good communicators
  - They can be persuaded to participate as session leaders

- The range of disciplines covered in your institution
- The geography of your institution and attendance patterns of active researchers

If this process leaves you with 500 enthusiastic applicants from many disciplines who just want to improve their success rates and 20 senior researchers willing to

---

lead sessions, you have one type of programme. If you have 15 research-active staff members keen to make their first application and an external leader who you can hire to come in and deliver a few sessions, you have another. Both are equally useful, but the style and content will vary. There is no 'one size fits all' solution for every research institution.

Depending on the profile of your institution, build your programme using some of the following formats. Which of them you choose to implement, in what combination and at what frequency will depend on your resources and the needs of your participants.

## Expert seminars

| | |
|---|---|
| Objectives: | To help researchers understand the evaluation process (*Process Stage 1*) |
| Speaker: | A distinguished academic who is well known within your institution and who has both extensive grants' committee experience and a strong track record of winning research funding |
| Venue: | Lecture theatre |
| Attendance: | No maximum |
| Format: | 40-minute presentation plus time for questions and discussion |
| Content: | This depends on how many events of this format you run. If you plan to offer just one or two sessions of this type, simply ask your speaker to tell participants what they have learned about grant-writing from sitting on grants' committees. The speaker should provide some insights into the experience of acting as a 'designated member' and ranking applications. If you can persuade them to mention the times that their own applications have been rejected, you will hear a collective sigh of relief from the attendees. If you plan to schedule a number of talks by different grants' committee members, try to theme each of them. There are plenty of topics to choose from and these tend to come up naturally in your initial discussions with the speaker. Possible examples include: 'the perfect case for support', 'what makes an application convincing', 'the life cycle of a grants' committee' or 'top 10 mistakes that applicants make'. |
| Timing: | Straight after lunch works well |
| Suitable for: | All potential applicants and research administrators |

| Caution: | Make sure that your speakers keep their advice as general as possible and do not take a multi-disciplinary audience through the working of one particular funding agency. |
|---|---|

## Themed workshops

| Objectives: | To help researchers make their research questions and projects stand out against others in the same competition (*Process Stage 2*) |
|---|---|
| Leader(s): | Researchers with grants' committee experience and a strong track record of winning research funding. If your institution covers a wide range of disciplines, you may wish to have two session leaders from different faculties leading this session jointly. Although the advice and insight of any grants' committee members is applicable to any discipline, this may be a counter-intuitive concept for participants and may affect sign-up. |
| Venue: | Seminar room with enough space for small group discussions |
| Attendance: | 10–20 participants |
| Format: | A workshop comprising brief introductions, short presentations by the leaders, plus group exercises, questions and discussion |
| Content: | You should design each session around the current needs or anxieties of your researchers and the knowledge and enthusiasm of the session leaders. Suitable themes might include: 'your first application', 'winning your second grant', 'large project grants', 'building collaborations', 'fellowship funding', or 'one idea, three applications'. If your institution relies on certain funding agencies for a large proportion of its grant income, you can also take an 'Inside X' theme led by committee members with support from regular referees and award holders. You can use the four propositions and some of the Tools from earlier chapters to design your group exercises. For example: |

- A 'fellowship' workshop might focus on the *competence* proposition and include some of the tools from Chapter 1 as group or paired exercises.
- A 'collaboration' workshop will focus on the *success* proposition and you could also use some of the advice and Tools from Chapter 13.

| Timing: | Two-hour workshop over lunch (provide sandwiches if you can) |
|---|---|

| | |
|---|---|
| Suitable for: | Every researcher in your institution, according to the theme |
| Caution: | Do not let participants dominate the session with technical queries about individual funding schemes. Refer these issues to research administrators who can arrange individual follow-up sessions so that discussions are not held up. |

# Grant-writing seminars

| | |
|---|---|
| Objectives: | To help researchers acquire the skills to write fundable research grant applications (*Process Stages 3 and 4*) |
| Leader(s): | Researchers with grants' committee experience, a track record of winning research funding plus strong teaching and mentoring skills. The leader should be prepared to speak from his or her own experience as an applicant. |
| Venue: | Informal seminar room |
| Attendance: | 10–20 participants |
| Format: | A presentation with hand-outs, examples of projects and applications, opportunities for structured discussion and questions. The presentation can be repeated regularly or used as a roadshow to different locations. |
| Content: | A brief overview of funding agency process and lots of practical advice on how to develop fundable applications. You can base this on Chapters 7, 9 and 10 of this book. In brief, your presentation should cover the following: |

- The funding agency evaluation process
- The four key propositions of fundable projects
- Generic application structure
- How agency templates work
- Generating evidence
- Making your application easy to read, easy to understand and convincing

| | |
|---|---|
| | This book will provide useful further reading for participants. |
| Timing: | Two-hour workshop |
| Suitable for: | Both inexperienced applicants and those who want to improve their success rate. In practice, you will find researchers at all levels attending these sessions. |
| Caution: | Do not let participants dominate the session with technical queries about individual funding schemes. Refer these issues to research administrators who may wish to attend workshops to make notes of specific queries so that discussions are not help up. |

# Application development workshops

| | |
|---|---|
| Objectives: | To support researchers as they develop individual projects from generating fundable ideas through to submission (*Process Stages 2 to 4*). Alternatively, you can just focus on *Process Stage 6* and how to generate frequent, high-quality applications. |
| Leader(s): | Researchers with grants' committee experience and a strong track record of winning research funding. If you choose to run Development Workshops, you will need someone with strong mentoring and motivational skills and the back-up of administrators who can help with the technical aspects of application development. |
| Venue: | Seminar room with enough space for small group discussions |
| Attendance: | 10–30 participants |
| Format: | A regular workshop series that participants attend while they are working on specific applications. This will depend on demand, your administrative resources and the profile of the institution. If your focus is on generating high-quality applications (*Process Stage 6*) quickly, you can run this as a one-off workshop. |
| Content: | Chapters 8 to 11 of *The Research Funding Toolkit* are a useful template for this series. You can run a sequence of events on 'generic structure', 'fitting the template', 'generating arguments and evidence' and 'writing skills' using the relevant advice and Tools as the basis of your exercises. These must be applied to live applications within the sessions and participants should have homework and objectives before the next session. If you are running a one-off *Process Stage* 6 workshop on generating high-quality applications quickly, applicants can attend with a research idea and a rough one-page summary of their project. |
| Timing: | This is flexible and you could have a rolling programme of monthly sessions or an intensive series linked to a particular deadline for a popular and demanding scheme. Each session should last no more than two hours. |
| Suitable for: | Committed, focused researchers who have less experience in making grant applications and minimal access to mentoring within their daily working environment. If participants are all working at the same pace it will help. This series works well in parallel with the other workshop events proposed in this chapter. |

| Caution: | Applicants do tend to work at different speeds so you need some flexibility to allow for occasional non-attendance and individual slow progress. This can be the most difficult type of event to run successfully with a very diverse group. |

## Application review panels

| Objectives: | To give participants the opportunity to obtain appropriate feedback and help them acquire the skills that allow them to give and receive feedback effectively (*Process Stage 5*) |
| Chair: | An experienced grants' committee member and quick thinker who can keep control of a fast-moving group exercise |
| Venue: | Meeting room with one big table |
| Attendance: | 4–8 |
| Format: | A simulation exercise of a grants' committee meeting using participants' current draft proposals |
| Content: | The organiser brings enough copies of the template form for each participant (see Test 11 in Chapter 11). The participants sit in a circle and pass their draft application to the person on their left. It helps if you are not sitting next to a person with whom you work closely. Everyone then has 15 minutes to read the relevant draft and prepare a short presentation using the template. This process feels pressurised and intense so there should be silence throughout to allow colleagues to concentrate. After 15 minutes, the group reconvenes. Each member of the group gives a two-minute presentation on their allocated application following the template guidance and is not allowed to make any quality judgements. Led by the Chair, the rest of the group (excluding the applicant) then has three minutes to ask questions, to which the presenter alone responds. The applicant must remain silent throughout this process. At the end of the presentations take some further time to discuss how well represented you felt by the busy non-specialists who took charge of your application and how it felt to work under these conditions. A brief explanation about how this process compares with a 'live' grants' committee by the Chair is also very useful. |
| Timing: | One to two-hour session (depending on numbers) over lunch. Provide sandwiches if you can. |

| Suitable for: | All potential applicants and research administrators |
| Caution: | Participants' applications do need to be at a reasonably advanced state (at a minimum, a complete draft of the case for support). You will have last-minute cancellations as applicants realise they cannot meet the deadline, so always over-recruit. |

# Organisation

Depending on the research profile of your organisation and the needs of your researchers, you will decide which of these events is right for you and how many of them to run.

The description of each template includes a note about possible pitfalls and areas that need careful management. There are also a few general points that you should keep in mind in order to keep your programme on track and ensure it is effective.

## 1 Attendance

It can be difficult to convince academic staff that training sessions may be of benefit. Busy, independent and sceptical, this group does not submit meekly to poorly-planned, time-wasting training events or corporate-style seminars.

This is why it is important that each event is hosted by a respected fellow researcher and that administrative input remains as invisible as possible. Equally, the titles of events should appeal to the target audience. The researchers you recruit to lead the sessions will usually have some ideas about this.

In order to encourage attendance, schedule the programme to suit the working patterns and preferences of attendees. If you work in an institution where many staff have childcare responsibilities, there is no point scheduling sessions for late afternoon. If researchers disappear for July and August or spend May marking exam papers, there is no point scheduling sessions during these months.

If you can keep sessions well below two hours and have the budget to provide sandwiches, lunchtime works well. The sandwiches are an incentive for those who have booked a place to actually turn up and the session does not intrude on the working day so obviously.

## 2 Administration

There is a considerable administrative load to organising events like these. Before you start make sure there is someone who can:

- Recruit and brief session leaders and help plan each individual event
- Help research and produce hand-outs and presentations
- Book rooms, prepare rooms and organise any refreshments
- Attend events to introduce speakers if necessary and deal with technical queries about individual research grants 'offline'
- Publicise events (using email, putting posters up of departmental notice boards, website news stories, blogs and social networking media)
- Recruit and brief participants (sending reminders, keeping lists, providing directions, informing them about advance preparation)
- Monitor attendance

You will usually need to plan and announce events several months ahead in order to ensure that session leaders and participants can fix the date in their diaries.

## 3 Speakers and session leaders

Once involved in an application development programme, most speakers and session leaders find the experience interesting and rewarding. The feedback can also be very flattering. However, these busy, senior researchers may need some incentive to get involved. You may also work in an institution with no one who fits the criteria or no one who is willing to help, whatever the incentive.

In either case, the simple option is to pay your session leaders – either with a fee or something in kind, such as teaching relief or some short-term research assistance.

If there is no one suitable within your organisation, you may find a suitable candidate from your external examiners, validating institution, collaborators of research staff or ex-PhD supervisors. This will probably be more expensive than using an 'insider', so you may need to use your speaker to maximum effect (e.g. *Expert Seminars*). You can then use some of the techniques in Chapter 11 in order to create structured self-help networks within the institution.

# APPENDIX 2

## THE APPLICATION TEMPLATE OVERVIEW

This book explains that applicants have a much better chance of submitting fundable grant applications when they understand the following:

- the knowledge level of referees and grants' committees
- the working conditions of referees and grants' committee members
- the specific evaluation criteria used by funding agencies to decide whether:
  - o your project asks an important question
  - o your project is likely to answer the question
  - o the likely gain from your project is worth the resources requested
  - o you are competent to carry out the project as described

Most schemes are assessed using the application document alone and how you present your research plans within the template provided is of crucial importance. In order to do this as effectively and efficiently as possible, it is helpful if you understand the function of each part of the application template and how the template is used by referees and grants' committee members.

As described in Chapters 7 and 8, most agency templates have underlying similarities that permit this generic approach and variations tend to be superficial. The two 'at a glance' tables summarise the similarities. The first provides an overview of the generic functions and the second shows how referees and grants' committee members will use the template.

## The generic functions of templates

The table below provides an overview of the generic functions of funding agency templates and should be used alongside agency guidance to decide what arguments and evidence you should include in each section of the template.

| Generic structure (see Chapter 7) | Which key propositions? (see Chapter 7) | Which template sections? | What content and evidence? | How to replicate, summarise or expand |
|---|---|---|---|---|
| Foot in the door | Use 'foot in the door' to show:<br><br>1 Importance<br>2 Success<br>4 Value | Summary<br>Abstract<br>Project Outline<br>Introduction<br>Background | Use all the information below to create a concise project summary after you have drafted the main narrative of your application:<br><br>1 State the main research question<br>2 Summarise the importance of the question<br>3 List the 3–5 things that 'we need to know'<br>4 Preview the project structure and principal resources<br>5 Summarise the outcomes | The summary relates to other parts of the template as follows:<br><br>1 Introductory sentences from each section of the main case for support narrative can be combined to provide the 'summary' section of the application template.<br>2 You can take the text from the 'summary' section of the application template and use it to introduce your case for support. |
| We have a problem | Use 'we have a problem' to show:<br><br>1 Importance<br>2 Success<br>3 Competence<br>4 Value | Introduction<br>Background<br>Rationale<br>Timeliness<br>State of the Art<br>Research Questions<br>Research Problems<br>Aims and Objectives<br>Track Record<br>CV | Use the information below to provide evidence for all four key propositions:<br><br>1 Restate the main research question<br>2 Provide evidence as follows:<br>  2a Why the problem needs solving | Include all the information from the previous column in the main case for support narrative. Then:<br><br>1 Rephrase research question and sub-questions as 'Aims and Objectives'.<br>2 Use CVs and/or Track Record section to reinforce self-citations in the 'we have a problem' section of the main narrative. |

| Generic structure (see Chapter 7) | Which key propositions? (see Chapter 7) | Which template sections? | What content and evidence? | How to replicate, summarise or expand |
|---|---|---|---|---|
| | | | 2b Why you have the skills and experience to solve the problem (using self-citation)<br>2c Why the project offers the best solution to the problem<br>3 Break the overall research question down into 3–5 sub-questions that combine to answer the main question. Provide evidence that:<br>3a We 'need to know' the answer to each sub-question<br>3b Your methods and approach to each sub-question are likely to succeed | |
| *This project is the solution* | Use 'this project is the solution' to show:<br>2 Success<br>3 Competence<br>4 Value | Research Methods<br>Plan of Investigation<br>Research Activity<br>Study Design<br>Work Packages<br>Dissemination<br>Outputs<br>Impact | The information below will usually be spread across several sections of the main case for support template and then expanded in appendices or the application form itself:<br>1 Restate the main research question | Provide an overall narrative within the main body of the case for support and include all relevant information in the previous column. Then:<br>1 Take each resource mentioned in (a) project budget and discussed in (b) case for support. Justify each |

*(Continued)*

(Continued)

| Generic structure (see Chapter 7) | Which key propositions? (see Chapter 7) | Which template sections? | What content and evidence? | How to replicate, summarise or expand |
|---|---|---|---|---|
| | | Public Engagement Exploitation Budget Justification of Costs Project Management Ethics Timetable Technical Annex | 2 Summarise overall approach and methods<br>3 Describe each activity component that corresponds to each sub-question and include specific, detailed information on:<br>  3a Methods and conduct<br>  3b Timing of activity<br>  3c All project/institutional resources<br>4 Describe the timetable of activity<br>5 Describe arrangements for project management<br>6 Include information on other funding agency requirements, such as public engagement or ethics<br>7 Include information on all project outputs | item fully in any (c) justification of costs appendix and ensure that all resources appear in all three sections.<br>2 Expand upon main case for support narrative in additional sections of the template devoted to dissemination (e.g. 'Impact', 'Exploitation', 'Public Engagement'). Ensure relevant resources are included in budget and mentioned in the main text.<br>3 Refer readers from main case for support to any appendices on methodology, ethics, etc.<br>4 Take information from main case for support on project timing and create a chart/table showing project timetable. |

# How templates are read and used

This table shows how different sections of the application template are used by different categories of referee and grants' committee member.

| Which Template Sections? | Referee | Designated Members of Grants' Committee | General Committee Member |
|---|---|---|---|
| Summary Abstract Project Outline Introduction Background | To get a preliminary idea of the structure of the proposal and note it down in preparation for reading the project in detail. To get the headings for the report:<br><br>What is the question?<br>Why it is important?<br>How does it answer the question?<br>What is the basic structure and scale of the project?<br>How will the results be disseminated? | To get a preliminary idea of the structure of the proposal and note it down in preparation for reading the project in detail. To get the headings for the oral presentation:<br><br>What is the question?<br>Why it is important?<br>How does it answer the question?<br>What is the basic structure and scale of the project?<br>How will the results be disseminated? | To get a rough idea of the project and decide whether the rest of it is interesting enough to read. |
| Aims and Objectives | To understand the structure of the research project, its components and potential outcomes. | To understand the structure of the research project and its components and potential outcomes. | For reference |
| Research Questions Research Problems | To understand how the research question breaks down into sub-questions that will be answered by activity components. | To understand how the research question breaks down into sub-questions that will be answered by activity components. | For reference |
| Background Rationale Timeliness State of the Art | To find out what evidence the applicants provide on how the project meets the funding agency's evaluation criteria (i.e. the four key propositions as interpreted by the agency). | They may speed-read this section (i.e. headings, section intros, the first sentences of some paragraphs). | For reference |

*(Continued)*

| Which Template Sections? | Referee | Designated Members of Grants' Committee | General Committee Member |
|---|---|---|---|
| Research Methods Plan of Investigation Research Activity Study Design Work Packages Project Management | To decide whether all the objectives can be met and the overall question answered. | They may speed-read this section (i.e. headings, section intros, the first sentences of some paragraphs). | For reference |
| Dissemination Outputs Impact Public Engagement Exploitation | To decide whether the project meets agency criteria for impact or user benefits and whether knowledge will be put to good use. | For reference | For reference |
| CV Track Record | To demonstrate the track record of the research team. | To demonstrate the track record of the research team. | To demonstrate the track record of the research team. |
| Budget | To see how much the project costs and why. | To see how much the project costs. | May refer to the overall cost. |
| Justification of Costs | To decide whether the project represents value for money. | For reference | For reference |
| Timetable | To decide whether the project is achievable and realistic. | For reference | For reference |
| Ethics/Compliance | Research ethics may be an evaluation criterion. | For reference | For reference |
| Referee Reports | N/A | To see what experts think of the project. The guidance may refer assessors to referee reports first. | For reference |
| PI Response to Referees | N/A | For reference, if any reviews seem unreasonable. | For reference |

# APPENDIX 3

## THE FUNDED APPLICATIONS: MORE INFORMATION

This appendix provides further information on the eight funded applications used as examples of good practice in this book.

They were chosen to represent a wide range of funding agencies, disciplines, project types, methodologies and career stage.

Some of the applicants have attended workshops run by the authors and others have run workshops and given talks on grant-writing themselves. Others have no connection with the workshops and are simply successful research grant applicants.

Although a set of eight applications can never be representative of the full range of funded research, the humanities, social sciences and sciences all feature among these case studies. The applicants range from those starting out in their academic careers through to internationally recognised researchers.

The projects themselves include travel grants, one- to five-year research projects, fellowships and large-scale collaborative programmes.

The funding agencies cover a number of different countries and include research councils, government agencies and a charity. None of the applications replicates every piece of advice in this book. However, all succeeded in producing stand-out project proposals that are easy to read, easy to understand and convincing.

A summary of each application follows:

## Digital Media Fellowship

**Title**: Language of the Interface
**Applicant**: Dr Aylish Wood
**Host Institution**: University of Kent, UK
**The Research Grant**: funding for a nine-month fellowship from the Arts and Humanities Research Council (AHRC). The grant included full salary replacement

for the Principal Investigator for the period of the project plus overheads, equipment, travel and funding for dissemination activity.

**Project summary from the original application**

We know moving image technologies evolve and proliferate. In technologically advanced societies moving images convey ideas and tell stories. But are we aware of the extent to which technological interfaces participate in shaping the language of moving images?

This interdisciplinary project draws from cinema studies, science and technology studies and software studies. Increasingly pervasive, animation is embedded in cinema, digital games, and commercial and educational websites. Animation's widespread and diverse impact makes it ideal to study the following questions:

Q. 1:  What does it mean to claim that technology participates or has agency in making images?
Q. 2:  Can a technological interface generate an audio-visual language?
Q. 3:  Does the language of an interface inform us about how our view of the world is evolving?

The project will be undertaken in four stages. Stages One and Three develop the theoretical ideas underlying the project: situated action and language of the interface. Stages Two and Four involve working with animations, games and web sites to expand and reflect on these theoretical insights.

## Stages One and Three: Defining Situated Action and the Language of the Interface

Science and technology studies offer a framework to define the key terms of this project. Bruno Latour argues that technologies have the potential to transform or mediate the ideas of image-makers. In a limited way technology can be understood to participate in the making of images. Lucy Suchman's work on situated action examines the hybrid agency that emerges in interactions between humans and technological interfaces. I use these two approaches to develop and introduce the 'language of the interface' as an analytic tool to explore how technological interfaces influence our understandings of the world.

## Stages Two and Four: Analysis of moving images and contextual materials

The theoretical frameworks will be used to explore moving image interfaces. These are divided into four categories: manipulation, play, proliferation, exploration. Each represents different situations. Manipulation focuses on creative work relying on manipulations of imagery, play addresses digital games, proliferation websites and exploration science-based animations.

My research method combines analysis of both moving images and contextual materials – published interviews and software manuals. Published interviews often unintentionally reveal information about complex interactions between practitioners and technology. Software manuals give insights into how interfaces are presented to practitioners.

Moving images studied include Wall-E, experimental works by UK-based animators SemiConductor. Games include Assassin's Creed and F.E.A.R. (Playstation 3), Echochrome (PSP), Flow (Playstation 3 on-line) and touchPhysics (iPod touch devices). Educational web sites to be accessed include science visualization web pages at Cold Spring Harbor and NASA.

My research will also be carried out through observation and interviews with image-makers. I am interested in learning how practitioners negotiate their way around the limits and possibilities of software packages. The material will be used as case studies to reflect on my theoretical ideas.

The participants have been selected on the basis that they cross the boundaries of entertainment and experimental animation, educational games and web sites, and as well as science visualizations. Potential contacts include Interactive Game Studio (Sweden), Institute of Play (US), and Wonky (UK).

## Dissemination

The research will be written up as 4 journal articles and presented at 3 conferences, including the Society of the Social Studies of Science, the Society for Animation Studies and Society for Cinema and Media Studies in 2011. A network for continuing dialogue with the animators will be established.

# Memory Research Project

**Title**: The Impact of Memory Reconsolidation on Vocabulary Acquisition: a Behavioural and Neural Investigation
**Applicant**: Dr Nicolas Dumay
**Host Institution**: Basque Center on Cognition, Brain and Language, Spain
**The Research Grant**: funding for a three-year research project from the MICINN (Ministry for Science and Innovation). The grant included funds for a full-ime research assistant, other staff, equipment and participant payments.

## Project summary from the original application

Traditional views of learning assume that new memories remain shaky for a short period, but soon *consolidate*, becoming resistant to interference from competing learning and amnesic agents (McGaugh, 2000).

However, recent – and not so recent – findings, mostly from animal neuroscience, suggest that this account is incomplete. These show that recalling a consolidated (and supposedly fixed) memory returns it temporarily to an unstable state, making it again susceptible to change until a new cycle of consolidation, or *reconsolidation* is achieved (Nader & Hardt, 2009).

This project bridges the gap between animal neuroscience and psycholinguistics, and looks at the impact of memory reconsolidation on word acquisition at the behavioural and neural levels. In this domain *consolidation* itself is a new concept. As Gaskell and I have shown, sleep plays a major role in feeding into our mental dictionary the words we learnt during the day (Dumay & Gaskell, 2007).

The present research examines the impact of reconsolidation at various levels of word acquisition. Experiments 1–5 are *behavioural* studies which look at the impact of reconsolidation on:

- Vocabulary list learning.
- The acquisition of words as motor sequences of syllables.
- The updating of lexical information.
- Lexical competition at the phonological and meaning levels.

Experiments 6–7 are *functional Magnetic Resonance Imaging* studies which identify the various brain areas involved in the learning, consolidation and reconsolidation of spoken word forms and their meaning.

All seven experiments follow the same logic. They assess the long-term retention of consolidated word knowledge, as a function of whether that knowledge is reactivated immediately before learning potentially corrupting information.

Findings will have strong implications for theories of human memory and models of language processing and acquisition, which all assume the stability of long-term representations. In addition, as this research introduces the idea that revising established knowledge shortly before learning similar information is ill-advised, results should also have substantial practical applications for (foreign) language tuition and remediation techniques.

## Theatre and Performance Visiting Fellowship

**Title**: Visiting Fellowship: Prof. Richard Schechner, New York University
**Applicant**: Prof. Paul Allain
**Host Institution**: University of Kent, UK
**The Research Grant**: a three-month Visiting Fellowship from the Leverhulme Trust, a UK charity dedicated to funding research from all disciplines. The grant included travel, a maintenance grant, technical support and some consumables.

**Project summary from the original application**

Professor Richard Schechner is as celebrated for his contribution to the founding of the field of Performance Studies as he is renowned for his influential work as a theatre director, most notably with the Performance Group in the 1960s and 1970s.

He has directed numerous collaborative pieces, several of them based on classical texts or adaptations of such, celebrated for their experimentation and political and social engagement as well as aesthetic risk. Many of these have been used as reference points for his own seminal theoretical studies of performance that have spanned four decades.

Our proposal is for Schechner to direct a devised production at Kent University in the Drama department in collaboration with staff and students. This is to enable Kent colleagues and practitioner/researchers to develop their own practice-as-research and theoretical studies to a higher level, by participating with and learning from a world-leading expert, whose career has always combined the close integration of practice and theory.

The emphasis on both lectures and the creation of a performance piece will allow research staff and students to follow through from start to finish a concrete and very specific research process based on preparation, realisation and dissemination through documentation and reflection.

# Research Animal Project

**Title**: Assessing the Welfare of Mice Used in Cancer Research
**Applicant**: Dr John Roughan, Dr Paul Flecknell
**Host institution**: Newcastle University, UK
**The Research Grant**: a three-year research project from the National Centre for the Reduction, Refinement and Replacement of Animal Use in Research (UK). The grant included research staff, laboratory equipment, consumables and travel and dissemination costs.

**Project summary from the original application**

The use of animals in medical research is a highly sensitive topic and in many cases the public perception is that this should not be allowed. Replacement strategies have been suggested such as culturing tumours outside of the body and then testing anticancer treatments. However, as scientists we know it is currently more appropriate to use animals as drugs [that] might combat cancer in people could behave very differently when tested in culture. Where animals are used we have a moral and legal obligation to minimise pain and suffering.

Animal cancer studies are an area where maintaining high welfare standards can be most challenging. We wish to obtain the highest quality scientific results whilst at the same time ensuring that the fewest animals suffer in the process. The key information we need to know is when pain occurs so that animals can be removed from studies prior to when they might begin to suffer. This is called determining the experimental 'end-point'. In a previous project we used behaviour changes as a method to assess when the animals might have begun to experience pain. This was partially successful in that we were able to identify changes that we think occurred because of pain. However we were unable to accurately determine how severe the pain was because we were not able to compare the results with equally accurate methods of determining how far cancer had progressed. In this new project we will use state-of-the-art scanning technology to regularly measure tumours whilst they are still growing within the body.

Humans are very different to other animals and human pain is a complex 'feeling'. Because of this some people speculate that animals might not be able to experience pain. They argue that animals could experience pain but it might not be something that actually matters to them. To convince them that they do experience pain, and that preventing it is something that we should take extremely seriously, we need to determine if they experience it in a way similar to us. A highly important aim of the work will be to determine whether pain affects them in the same way that it does humans with cancer. This will be achieved using tests designed to allow the mice to tell us how they are feeling. We will monitor whether they seek to obtain pain killing drugs when they are given a choice to do so. Being in pain and not are 2 very different feelings in humans. If these 2 very different states are also 'felt' by mice, then we should be able to train them to perform different tasks to obtain food rewards. How well they learn to complete simple tasks will tell us if they are able to 'feel' pain.

The outcomes of this project will help to improve the abilities of researchers to assess and prevent pain in mice involved in cancer research, and so should have a positive impact upon the welfare of a large numbers of animals. The results of the work will be in the public domain, and will show that concern for the welfare of research animals is a prime concern of the researchers involved.

## Rendition and Detention Project

**Title:** The Globalisation of Rendition and Proxy Detention
**Applicants:** Dr Ruth Blakeley, Dr Sam Raphael
**Host Institutions:** University of Kent, Kingston University, UK
**The Research Grant:** An eighteen-month Economic and Social Research Council (ESRC) project. The grant included investigator time and dissemination activity.

**Project summary from the original application**

This project asks how the extraordinary rendition and proxy detention of terror suspects have developed and whether they are US-led phenomena.

Although highly secretive by nature, substantial documentary evidence shows that terror suspects are transferred illicitly to other states, where they may be tortured. It is generally assumed that the global system of rendition and proxy detention is US led, but early evidence suggests that it may be much more diffuse. It also appears to be operating differently in the three regions most involved (Asia, the Middle East and Africa), and localised systems of rendition and proxy detention may pre-date the 'War on Terror'.

Our understanding of rendition is based on work by human rights NGOs and investigative journalists. This gives us some knowledge of the roles of the US and UK. However, scholarly inquiry to date tends to focus on the legal aspects. There has been very little analysis on the states that provide proxy detention, or how the system operates globally.

This eighteenth-month study will develop a theoretical model for rendition and proxy detention using three case studies of representative 'proxy' states in Asia, the Middle East and Africa. Sources will include as yet unanalysed databases of detention facilities and detainees and the case histories will enable the research team to provide a more robust theoretical basis for this illicit yet widespread phenomenon. In particular, the project will explore three key aspects of the process:

1. Whether the rendition and proxy detention system is hierarchical and US-led.
2. Whether the US is co-opting local and autonomous mechanisms.
3. Whether the system is diffuse, involving networks and collaborations between multiple states.

Findings from this project may challenge public assumptions about rendition and proxy detention as a US response to the 'War on Terror'. The development of a theoretical model will contribute to scholarly debate on security collaborations and state terrorism. Project outputs will also be of practical use to those agencies and individuals involved in legal and human rights' opposition to the practice.

# Web Authoring Project

**Title**: SWAT (Semantic Web Authoring Tool)
**Applicants**: Dr Richard Power, Prof. Donia Scott, Prof. Alan Rector, Dr Robert Stevens
**Host institutions**: Open University, The University of Manchester
**The Research Grant**: funding for a three-year research project from the Engineering and Physical Sciences Research Council (UK). The grant included

two post-doctoral research associates, a project student, travel, dissemination, equipment and meeting costs.

**Project summary from the original application**

During the last decade the Semantic Web community has established basic standards for representing data and the conceptual systems (ontologies) through which they are defined. However, encoding information in these formalisms (OWL, RDF) remains a technically difficult task. Widespread adoption of these technologies (with their important potential benefits) would be facilitated if transparent interfaces to the technical formalisms were available.

The project aims to show that metadata in OWL and RDF can be viewed and authored through computer-generated presentations in natural languages (e.g., English). The crucial step theoretically will be to develop a model for systematically mapping logical concepts and relations to phrase patterns in natural language. The practical challenge will be to develop a tool through which ontology developers can specify this mapping, without deploying deep knowledge of ontologies or grammars. This tool will draw on existing wide-coverage linguistic resources, so that developers can select from a range of pre-coded patterns rather than having to define new ones. If successful, the project would provide an innovative solution to an urgent and commercially relevant problem (as shown by the letters from our collaborators). The main partners are leading UK experts in the theory and practical application of ontologies (Manchester University), and the design of easily-used tools for knowledge-editing based on generated text (Open University).

# Software Testing European Project

**Title:** ProTest: Property-based Testing
**Applicants:** Prof. John Derrick (Sheffield), Prof. Simon Thompson (Kent), Dr Lars-Åke Fredlund (UPM), Prof. John Hughes (UGOT/Chalmers/Quviq), Prof. Thomas Arts (Chalmers/Quviq), Anders Kaspár (Ericsson AB), Francesco Cesarini (Erlang Solutions), Victor Gulias (LambdaStream)
**Host institutions:** University of Sheffield (co-ordinating institution, UK), University of Kent (UK), Universidad Politécnica de Madrid (Spain), University of Göteborg (Sweden), Chalmers University of Technology (Sweden), Ericsson AB, Erlang Solutions, Quviq AB, LambdaStream
**The Research Grant:** a three-year European Commission Framework Programme 7 STREP ('small or medium-scale focused research project') collaborative project. The grant included investigator time plus funds to support

employment of research staff, innovation activity, dissemination, software, equipment and project management.

**Project summary from the original application**

This project will develop software engineering approaches to improve reliability in Pervasive and Trusted Network and Service Infrastructures (ICT-2007.1.2). This is achieved today by extensive testing, combined with monitoring and logging in the field. Volumes of automated tests and logging code are written, failures must be analysed and diagnosed – and this accounts typically for half the cost of software. Even so, residual errors impose high costs on users.

We aim to automate much fault-finding and diagnosis, reducing its cost and improving effectiveness, based on properties of the system (specified by developers) which should always hold. Automated tools will generate and run tests, monitor execution at run-time, and log events for post-mortem analysis. When properties fail, the tools will search for simplest failing cases, and analyse trace and coverage information, to assist speedy diagnosis. Concurrency is a major challenge, which will be addressed in part by integrating model checking into our tools. Today's developers are not used to formulating general properties, so we will investigate ways of deriving them from two sources: UML (or UML-like) models, and by refactoring existing test suites. We combine academic expertise in refactoring, model-checking and testing; a tool vendor; and industrial expertise in telecoms. Three partners are SMEs; Ericsson is a leading telecoms supplier. All use Erlang, an open-source concurrent functional language aimed at telecoms and internet servers, which will be a common vehicle for our research – easing the transfer of theory into industrial practice. Erlang's good interoperability will enable our tools to find faults in all kinds of systems.

Our results will improve our tool vendor's products, be adopted by our partners within Ericsson and LambdaStream, and be disseminated by ETC to their customers throughout Europe's telecoms sector. This three-pronged strategy will guarantee real impact.

**Project website**: www.protest-project.eu

# Spoken Word Project

**Title**: Development and Redevelopment of Lexical and Sub-Lexical Representations
**Applicant**: Prof. Arthur Samuel
**Host institution**: Stony Brook University, USA

**The Research Grant**: a five-year research project National Institute of Child Health and Human development (US National Institutes of Health). The grant included investigator time, a research team and direct research expenses.

## Project summary from the original application

Understanding language is one of the most fundamental human cognitive abilities. It plays an important role in normal development, and is the major means for acquiring information in many domains. A number of psychological disorders (e.g., schizophrenia) can disrupt the normally impressive functioning of this system, greatly exacerbating the negative consequences of these disorders. Psycholinguists have made significant progress in clarifying the structures and processes that underlie language comprehension. Despite this progress, much remains to be learned about how words are represented in a person's 'mental lexicon'. Critical remaining issues in this area revolve around questions of <u>lexical representation</u>, and <u>lexical access</u>. Theories must specify how the presentation of a spoken word leads to a particular lexical representation becoming activated, and what the effects of such activation are: What effect does one active lexical representation have on others, and on units at other levels of representation?

The current proposal includes a large set of theoretically-driven empirical studies of lexical activation. The empirical investigations are organized into three interlocking groups of experiments. One set of studies examines how phonetic variation can affect lexical access, and can even change the lexical representations themselves. Such variation can have surprisingly powerful effects on how words are represented in the lexicon. A second set of studies examines even more fundamental changes in the lexicon: How do adults add new items to their mental lexicons, and what are the consequences of such changes? The third set of experiments investigates the dynamics of lexical competition: How does the activation of one lexical item affect the activation levels of other lexical entries?

The product of the proposed research will be a much better understanding of the architecture of the system that accomplishes language comprehension. These studies will provide a much more detailed picture of how the mental lexicon changes over both the short term and the longer term. Such an understanding is critical to our understanding language processing. In turn, because language is such a fundamental cognitive ability, progress in describing language processing will enhance our understanding of human cognition, under both normal and disordered conditions.

# INDEX

Grants' committee *cont.*
 source of insider knowledge 27
 also see *decision makers*
Grants, see *research grants*

H

Headings 133
sub-headings 126–127

I

Ideas x
 avoiding idea exhaustion 23, 39
 generating project ideas 37, 39–40, 180
 matching ideas to funding agencies 40
 also see *tests*
Impact – social and economic 16, 21, 89, 99,
  100, 103–105, 116
Importance proposition 30, 51, 75, 82, 108,
  114, 121–122
 collaborative projects 172
Institutional support 19, 29, 31–34,116
Introduction, see *'foot in the door'*
Isolation 27, 31–33

J

Justifying costs 157–158
also see *budget*

K

Key propositions, see *four key propositions*

L

Labelling 119, 126–127, 129
Language, see *writing skills*
Layout 95,129–133,142
Leverhulme Trust 3, 5, 54, 166
Linking 125–126, 129
Literature review 27, 82–89
Lone scholars 8
Luck
 good and bad ix,15, 19–20, 23, 23, 43,
  45, 109
 multiple applications 37
 lottery ticket 38

M

Medical Research Council (MRC) 20, 96
'Memory Research Project' 79, 84, 104, 125,
  127, 197–198
Methodology 45, 48, 57, 89, 90,
  91, 115, 173
 also see *success proposition*
Mistakes, made by grant-writers 107
MRC, see *Medical Research Council*
Multiple applications

check success rates when planning 38
creating efficiencies 42
main obstacles 74–75

N

National Institutes of Health 20, 54
Natural Environment Research Council
  (NERC) 96
Networking 27–35, 41, 138, 164–5
Nuffield Foundation 20, 98

O

Office politics – how to deal with 65–72
Online application templates 22

P

PDRAs, see *postdoctoral research fellows*
Peer review ix
 choosing referees 56
 criteria 57–58
 expertise 4
 how referees work 57
 informal peer review 29, 34, 41
 reports ix
 role of referees 50
 also see *decision makers*
 also see *assessment*
PhD students 67,143,145,154
Pilot data 15, 114
Planning applications 22, 39
 suggested timeline 46–47
 time management 47–48
 also see *deadlines*
Post-doctoral research associates 152–153
Priming 119, 121
 in relation to signposting 124
 priming the investigators 123
 priming the problem 122
 priming the question 121–122
 priming the resources 123
Principal Investigator 6, 8, 10, 137, 155
 also see *applicants*
Project ideas, see *ideas*
Project management 7, 57, 58, 95, 100–101,
  102–103, 115
Project structure 75, 87, 88–89
Proposal, see *case for support*
Propositions, see *four key propositions*
Public engagement 99, 100, 103–105, 116,
  192, 194
Publications 7, 11, 12
 collaborative research 164–165
 demonstrating research independence 8
 Principal Investigator 6
 also see *track record*